KING ARTHUR AND THE KNIGHTS OF THE ROUND TABLE

by M. C. Hall

illustrated by C. E. Richards

LIBRARIAN REVIEWER
Allyson A.W. Lyga MS - Library Media/Graphic Novel Consultant

READING CONSULTANT
Mark DeYoung - Classroom Teacher

www.raintreepublishers.co.uk
Visit our website to find out more information about Raintree books.

To order:
Phone +44 (0) 1865 888066
Fax +44 (0) 1865 314091
Visit www.raintreepublishers.co.uk

Raintree is an imprint of Capstone Global Library Limited, a company incorporated in England and Wales having its registered office at 7 Pilgrim Street, London, EC4V 6LB – Registered company number: 6695582

"Raintree" is a registered trademark of Pearson Education Limited, under licence to Capstone Global Library Limited

First published by Stone Arch Books in 2007
First published in hardback in the United Kingdom in 2009

Art Director: Heather Kindseth
Cover Graphic Designer: Heather Kindseth and Kay Fraser
Interior Graphic Designer: Heather Kindseth

Edited in the UK by Laura Knowles
Printed and bound in China by Leo Paper Products Ltd

ISBN 978-1406212488 (hardback)
13 12 11 10 09
10 9 8 7 6 5 4 3 2 1

British Library Cataloguing in Publication Data
Hall, Margaret, 1947-
King Arthur & the knights of the Round Table. -- (Graphic revolve)
741.5-dc22
A full catalogue record for this book is available from the British Library.

TABLE OF CONTENTS

Introducing (Cast of Characters) 4

Chapter 1 6

Chapter 2 20

Chapter 3 26

Chapter 4 34

Chapter 5 44

Chapter 6 49

INTRODUCING . . .

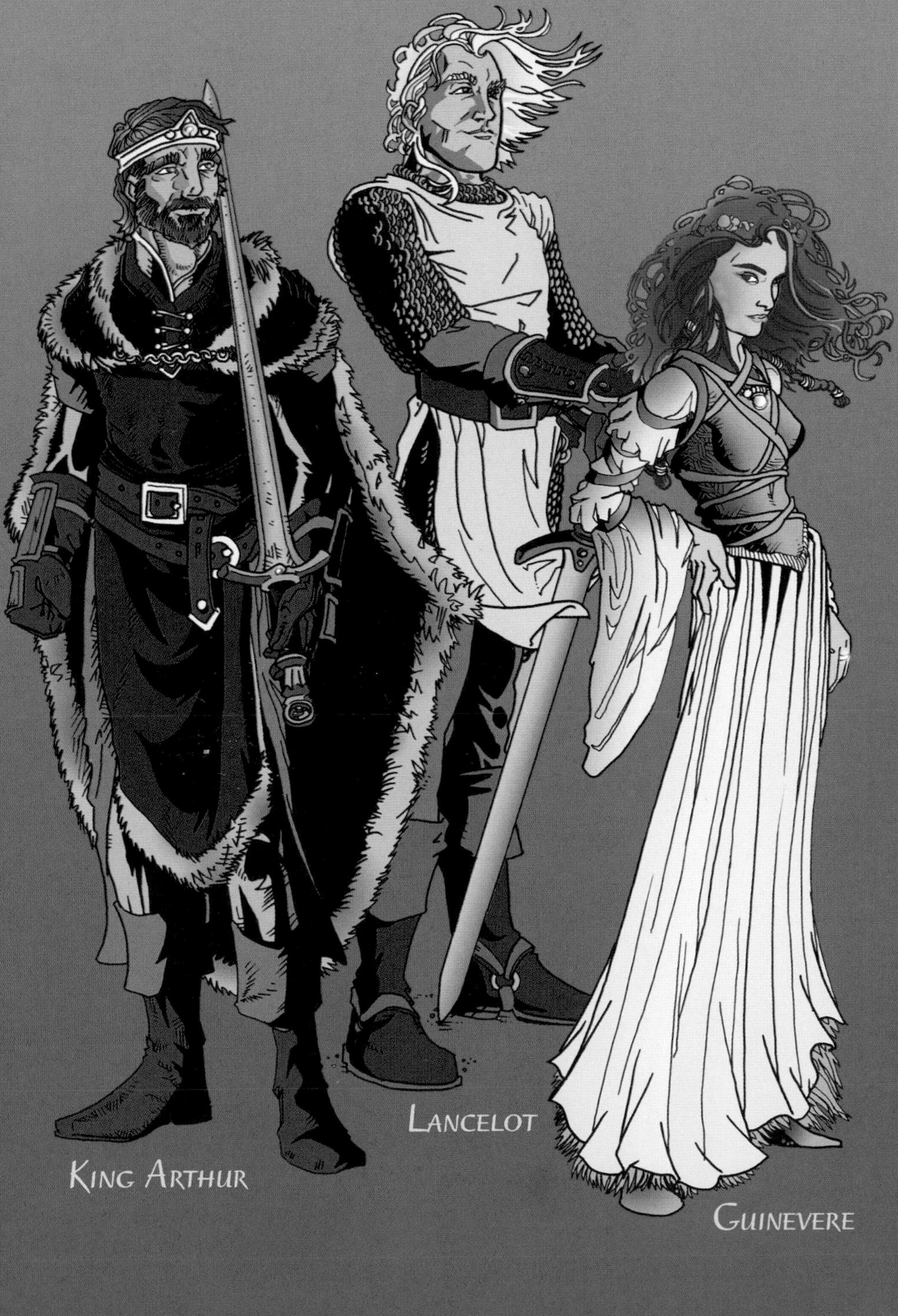

King Arthur
Lancelot
Guinevere

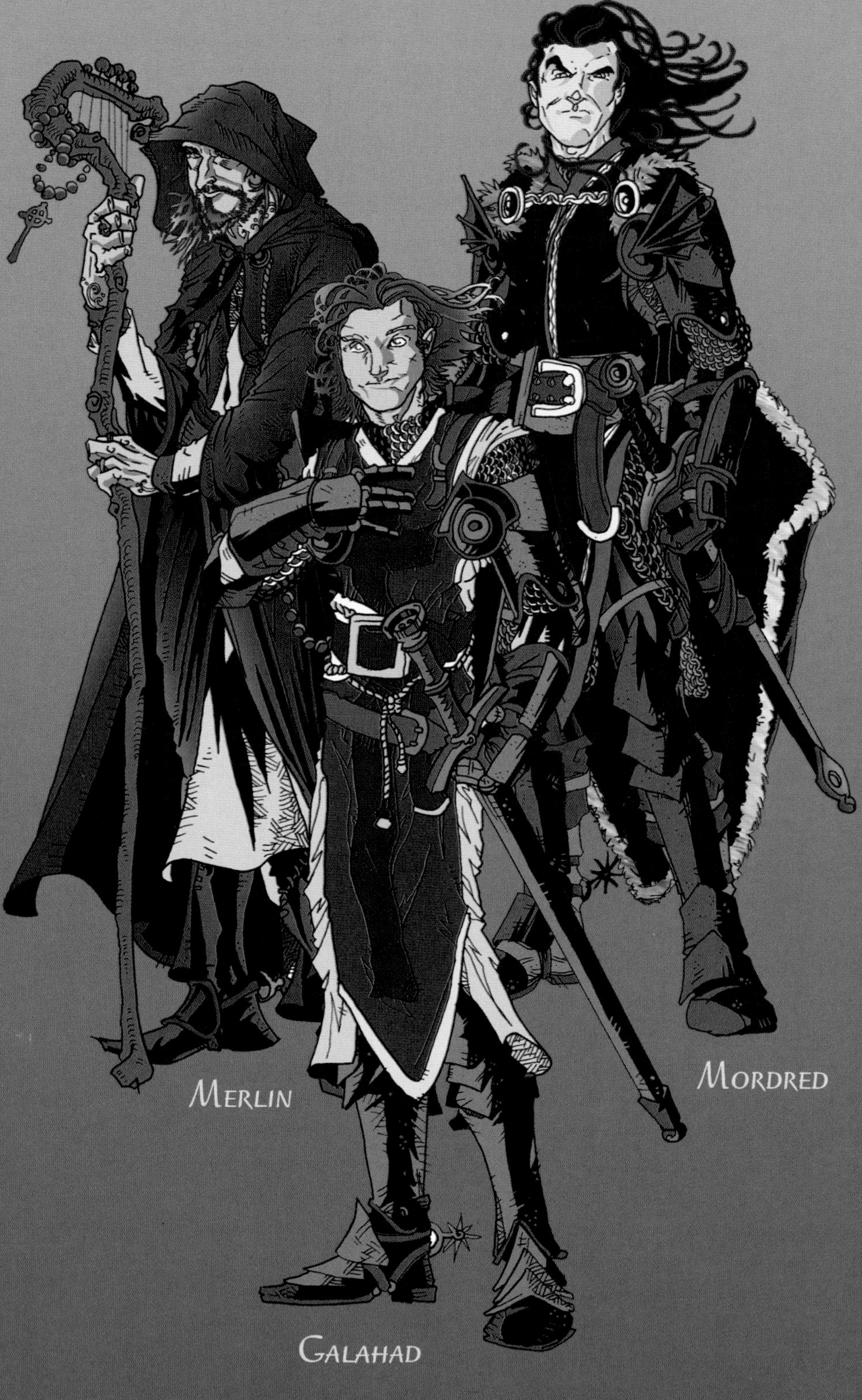
Merlin
Mordred
Galahad

CHAPTER 1

Long ago, in a dark time, two mighty armies fought.

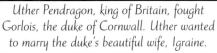

Uther Pendragon, king of Britain, fought Gorlois, the duke of Cornwall. Uther wanted to marry the duke's beautiful wife, Igraine.

I would give anything to beat my enemy.

Anything, my lord?

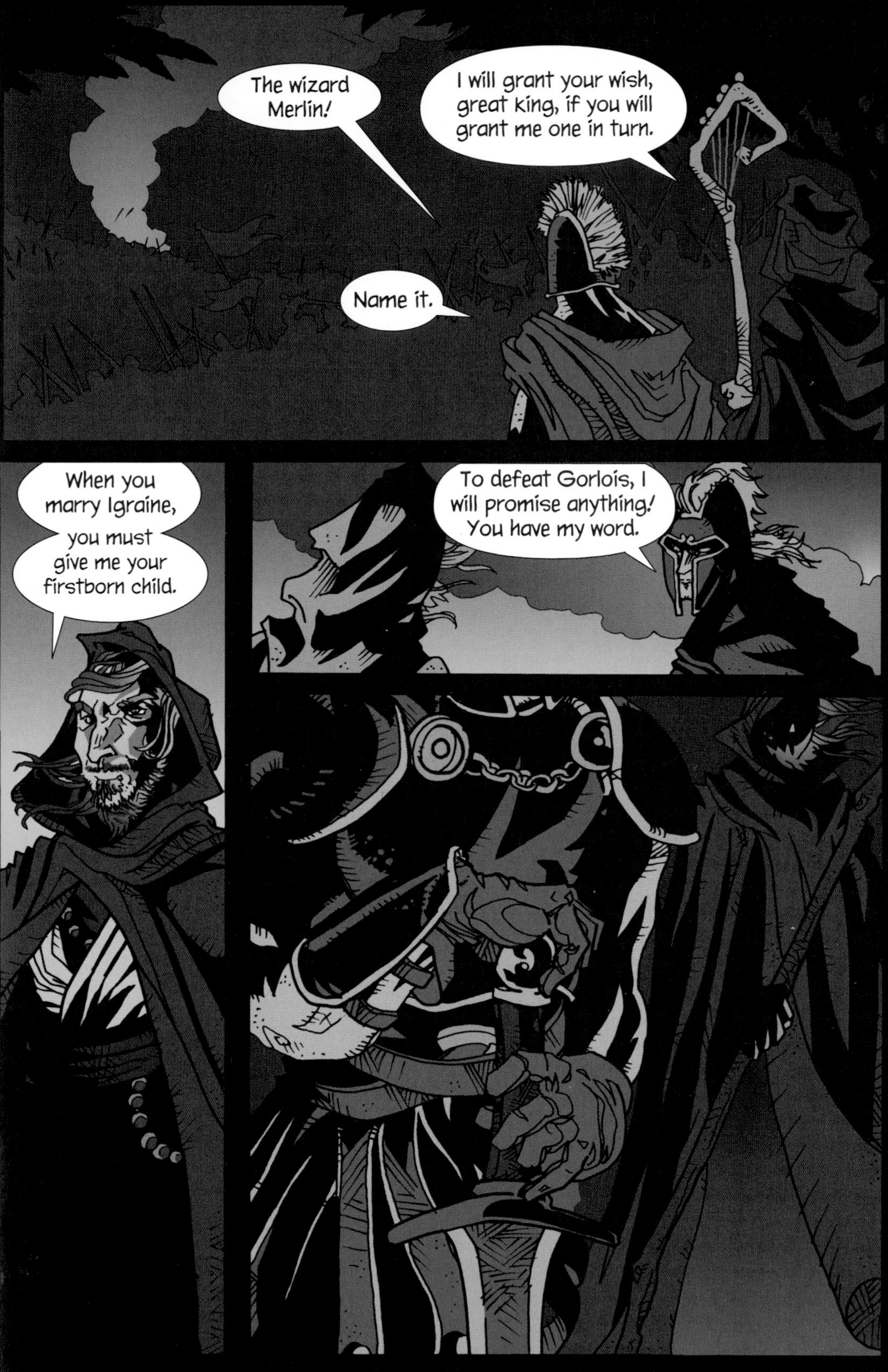
The wizard Merlin!
I will grant your wish, great king, if you will grant me one in turn.
Name it.
When you marry Igraine,
you must give me your firstborn child.
To defeat Gorlois, I will promise anything! You have my word.

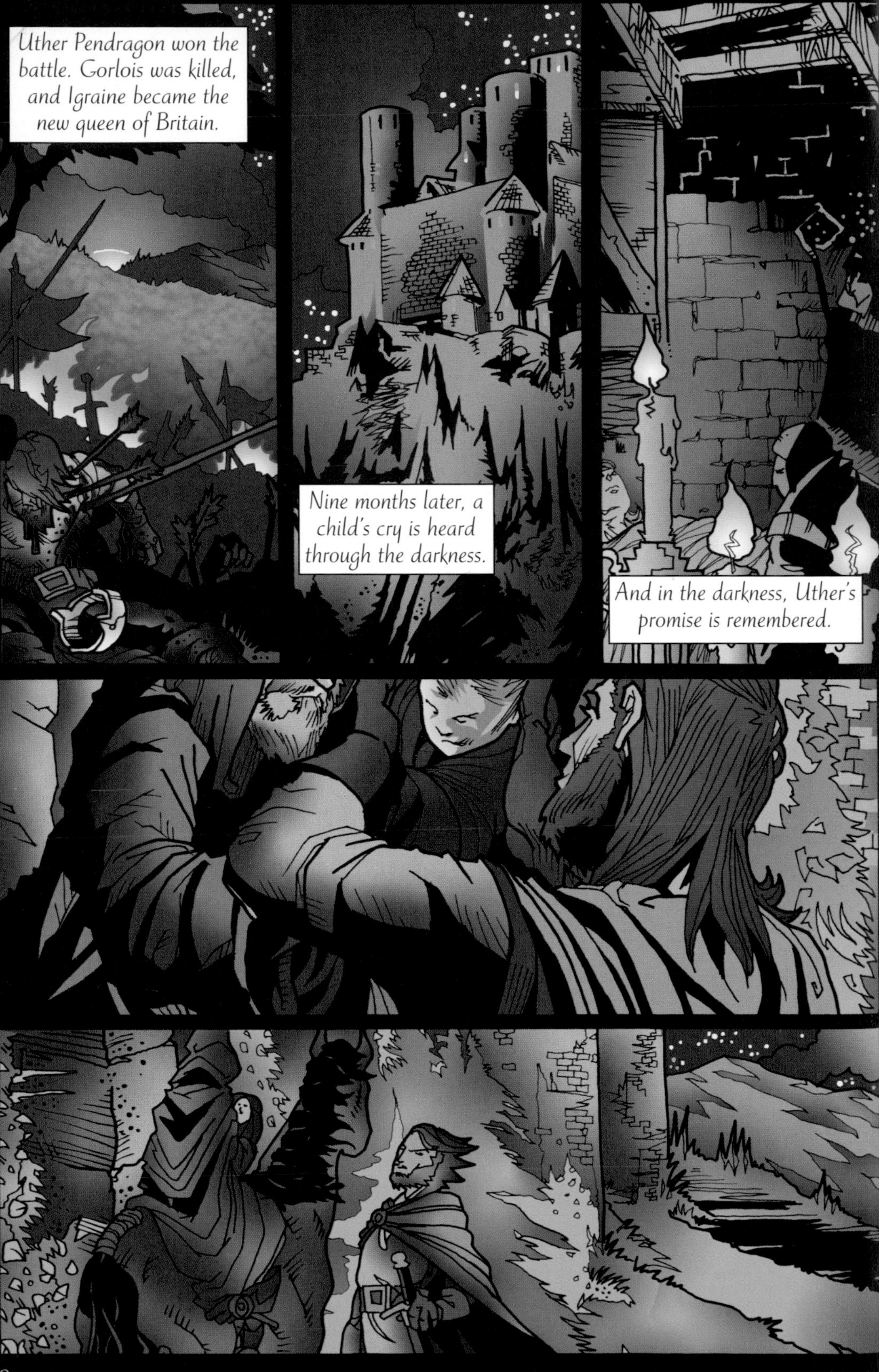
Uther Pendragon won the battle. Gorlois was killed, and Igraine became the new queen of Britain.
Nine months later, a child's cry is heard through the darkness.
And in the darkness, Uther's promise is remembered.

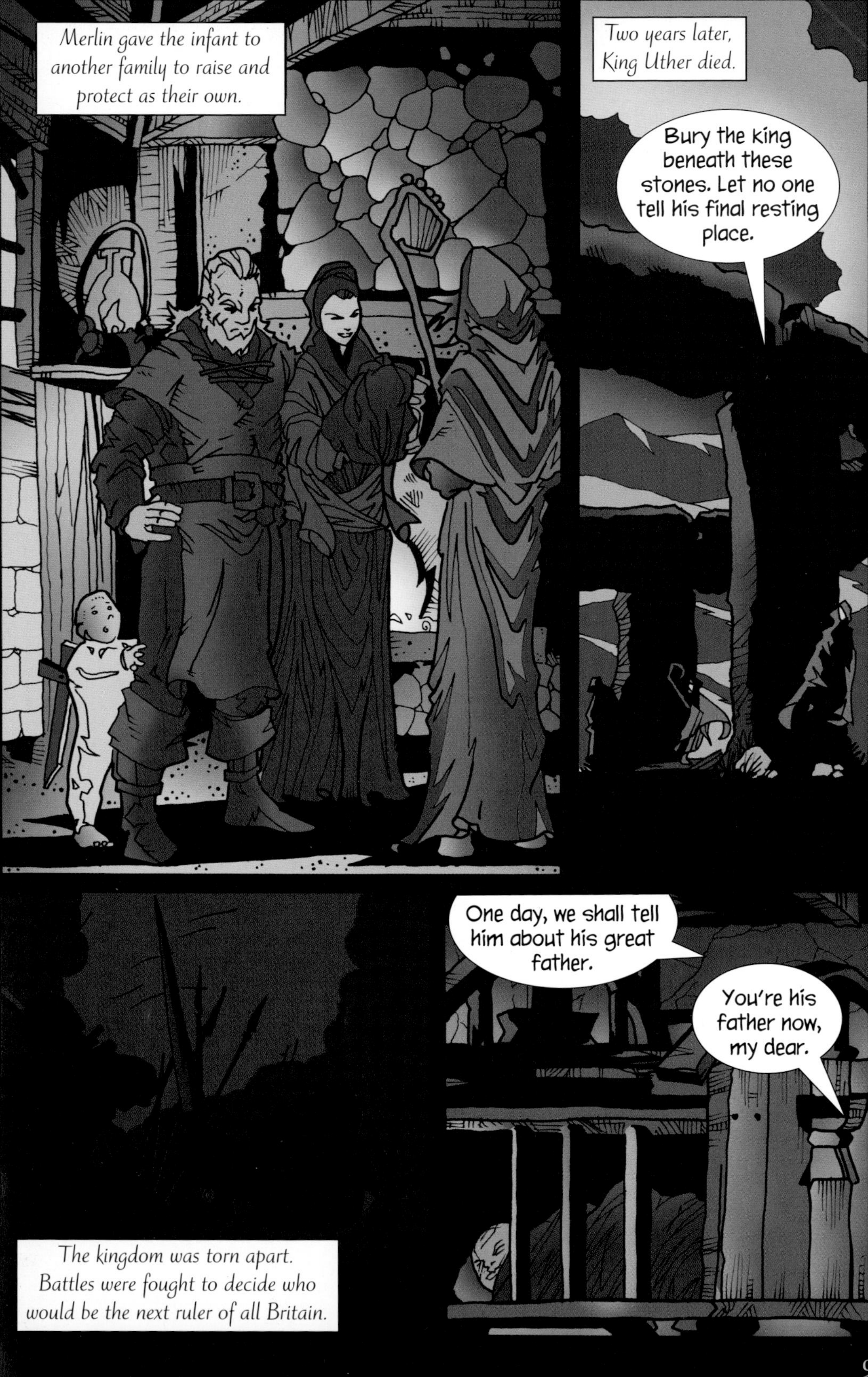
Merlin gave the infant to another family to raise and protect as their own.
Two years later, King Uther died.
Bury the king beneath these stones. Let no one tell his final resting place.
The kingdom was torn apart. Battles were fought to decide who would be the next ruler of all Britain.
One day, we shall tell him about his great father.
You're his father now, my dear.

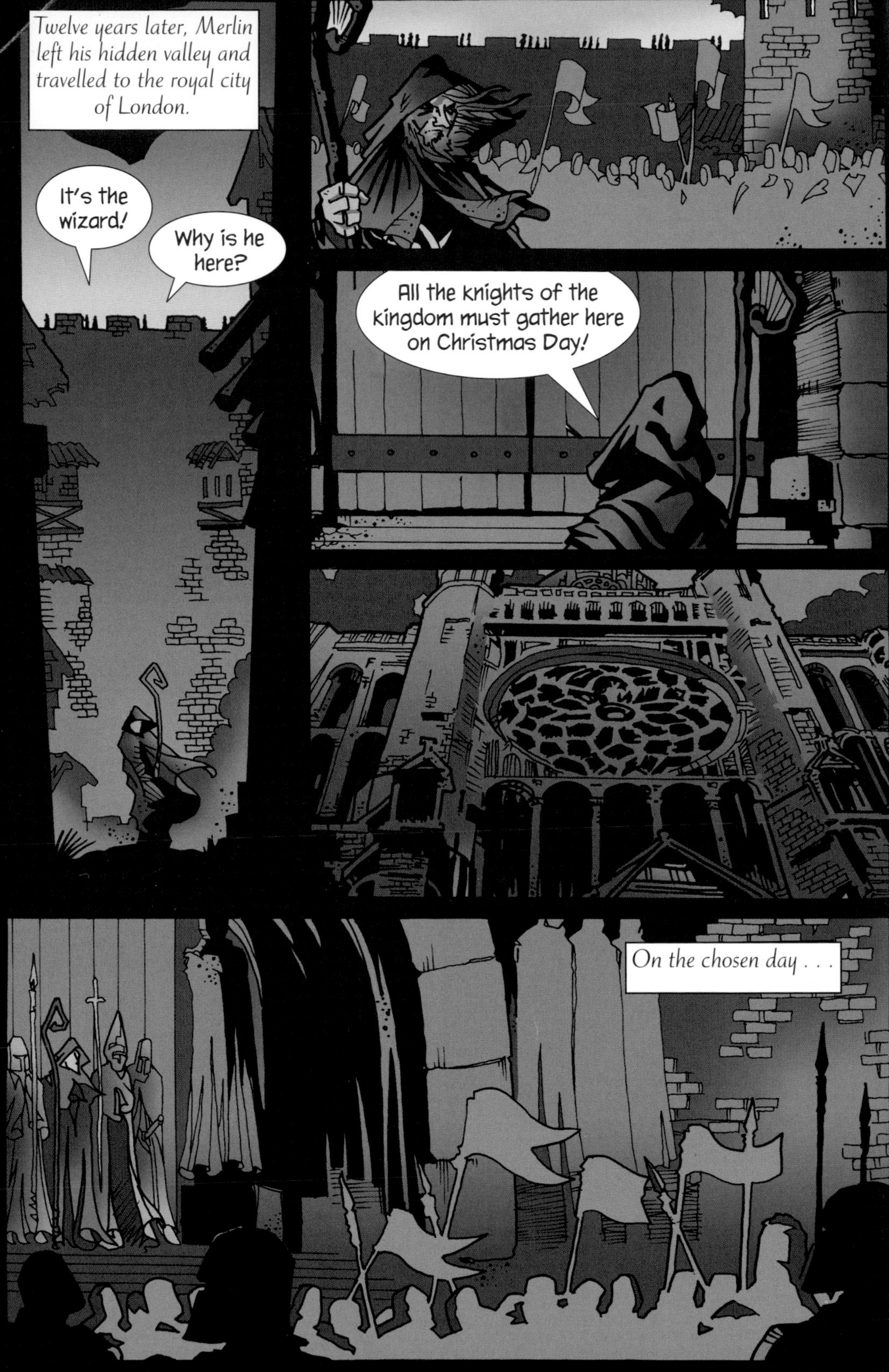

Twelve years later, Merlin left his hidden valley and travelled to the royal city of London.
It's the wizard!
Why is he here?
All the knights of the kingdom must gather here on Christmas Day!
On the chosen day . . .

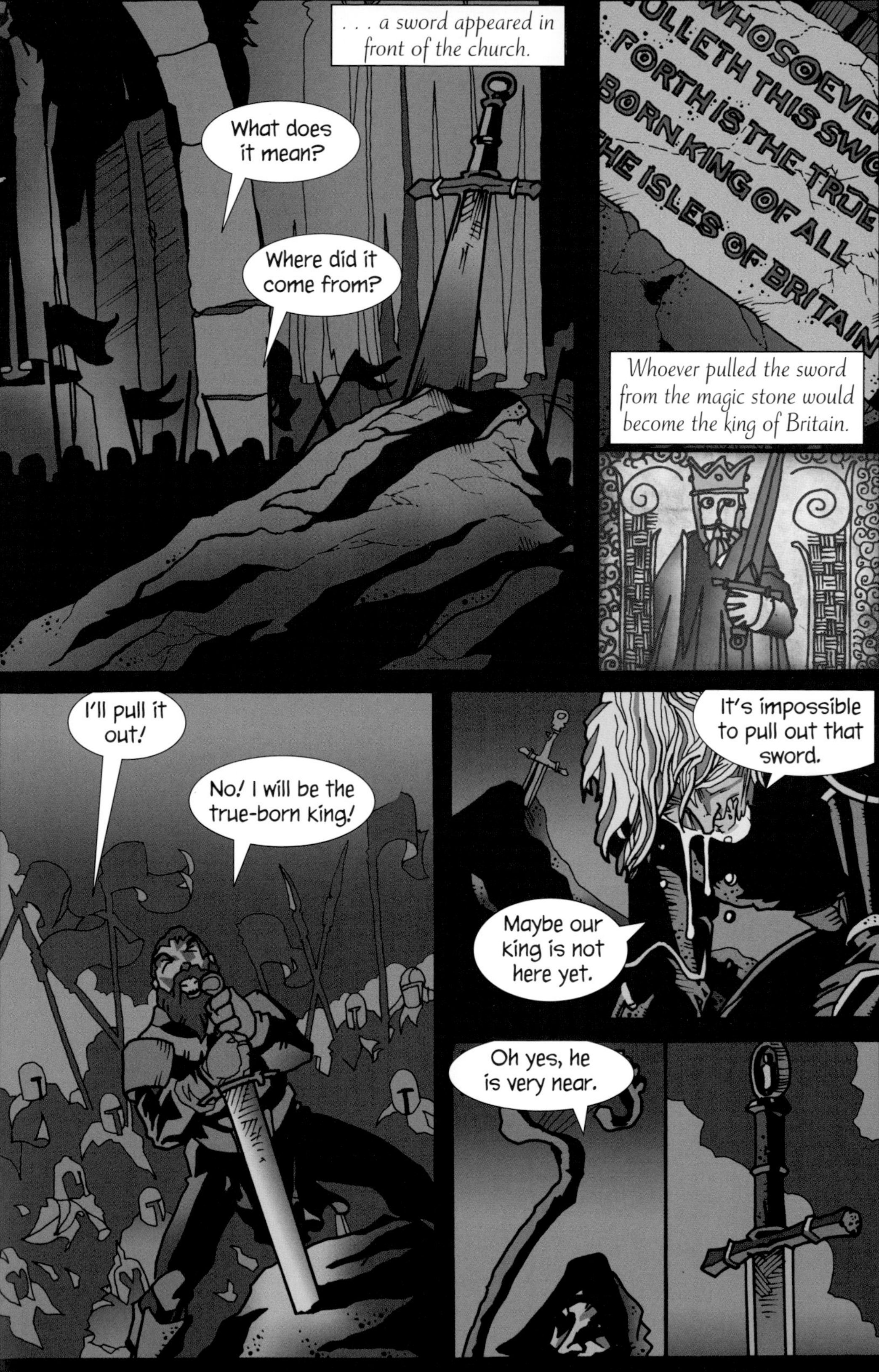

. . . a sword appeared in front of the church.
What does it mean?
Where did it come from?
WHOSOEVE
ULLETH THIS SWO
FORTH IS THE TRUE
BORN KING OF ALL
HE ISLES OF BRITAIN
Whoever pulled the sword from the magic stone would become the king of Britain.
I'll pull it out!
No! I will be the true-born king!
It's impossible to pull out that sword.
Maybe our king is not here yet.
Oh yes, he is very near.

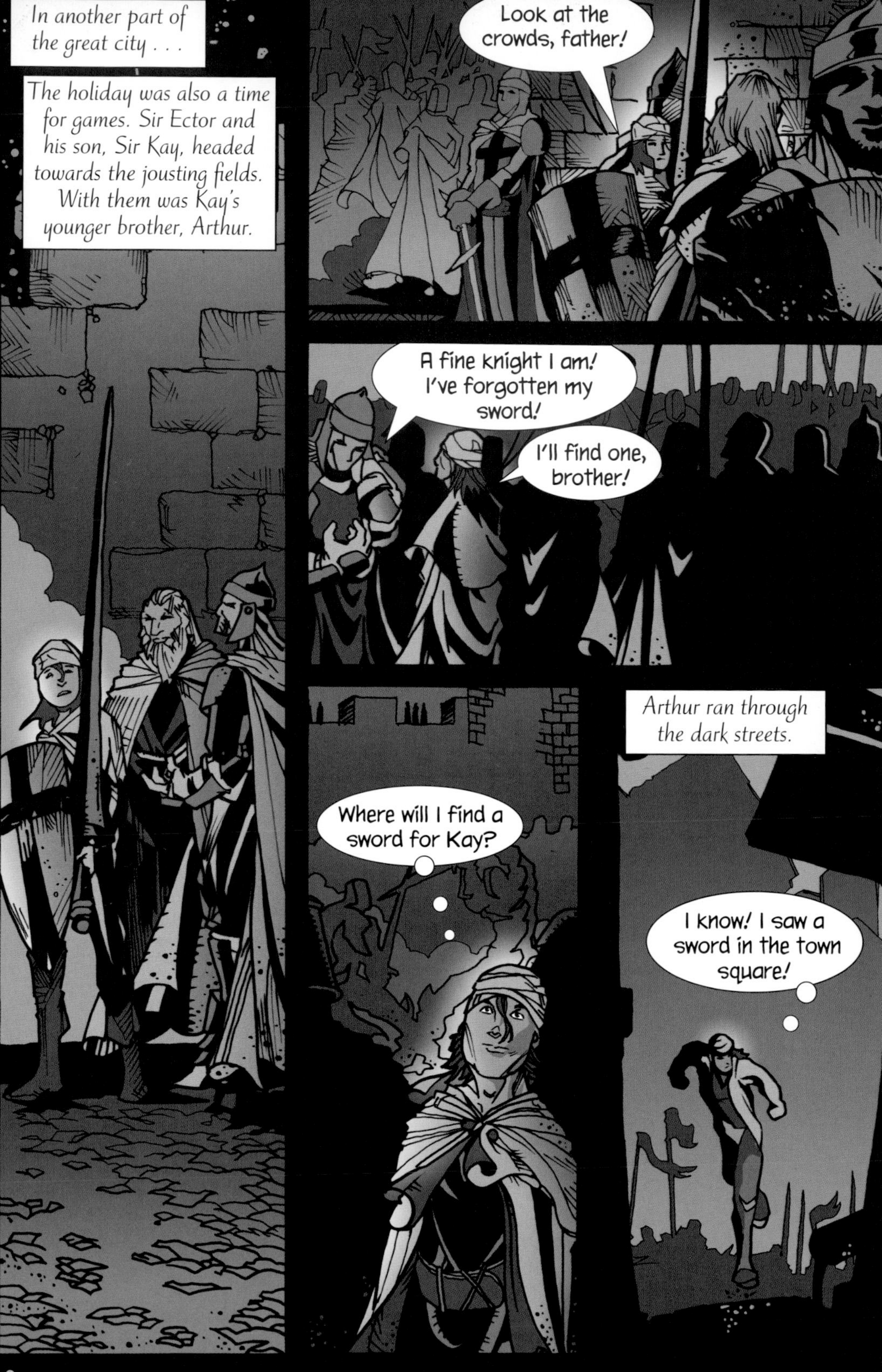
In another part of the great city . . .
The holiday was also a time for games. Sir Ector and his son, Sir Kay, headed towards the jousting fields. With them was Kay's younger brother, Arthur.
Look at the crowds, father!
A fine knight I am! I've forgotten my sword!
I'll find one, brother!
Where will I find a sword for Kay?
Arthur ran through the dark streets.
I know! I saw a sword in the town square!

Arthur was in too much of a hurry to read the words on the stone.

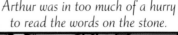

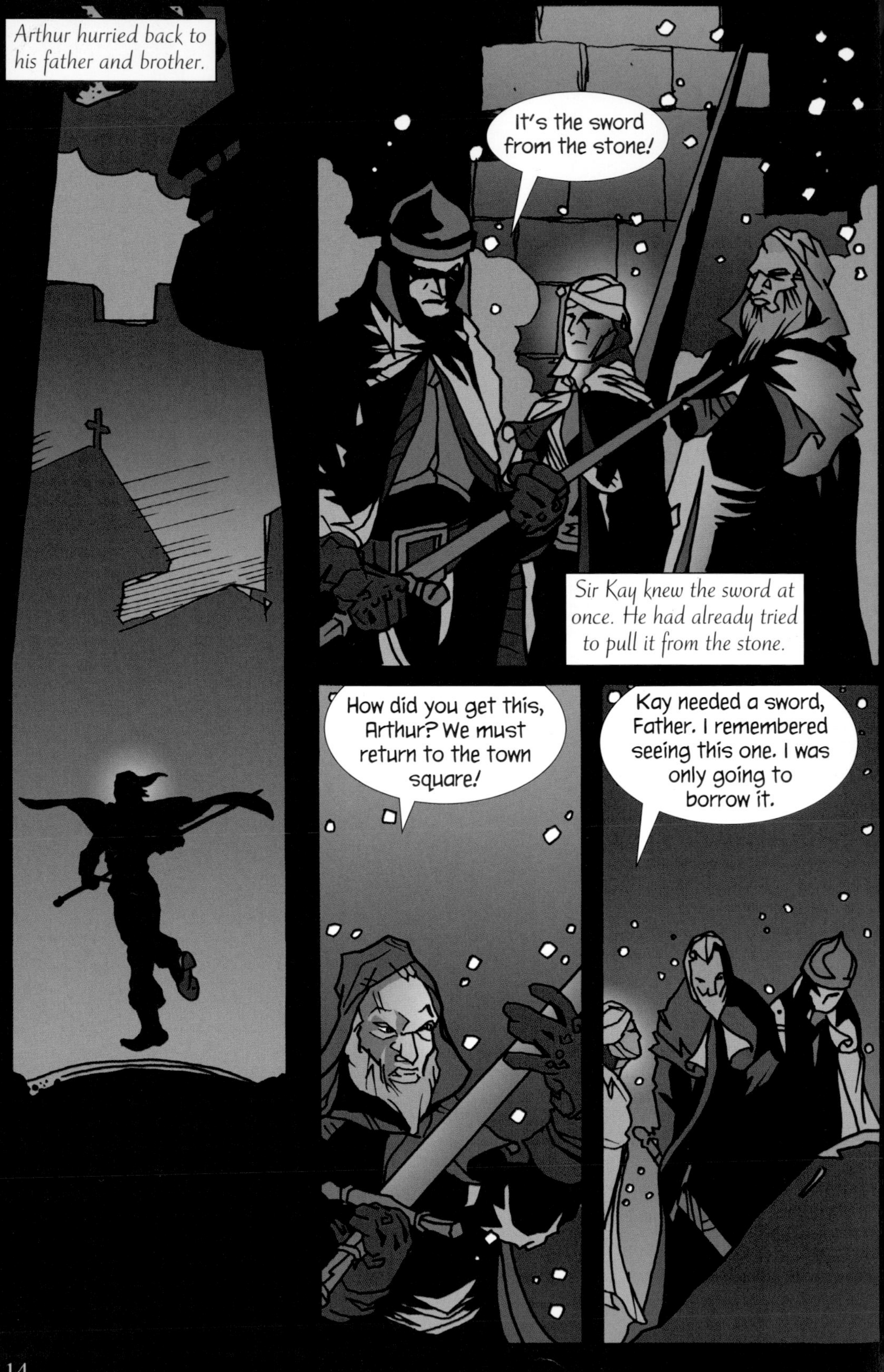

Arthur hurried back to his father and brother.
It's the sword from the stone!
Sir Kay knew the sword at once. He had already tried to pull it from the stone.
How did you get this, Arthur? We must return to the town square!
Kay needed a sword, Father. I remembered seeing this one. I was only going to borrow it.

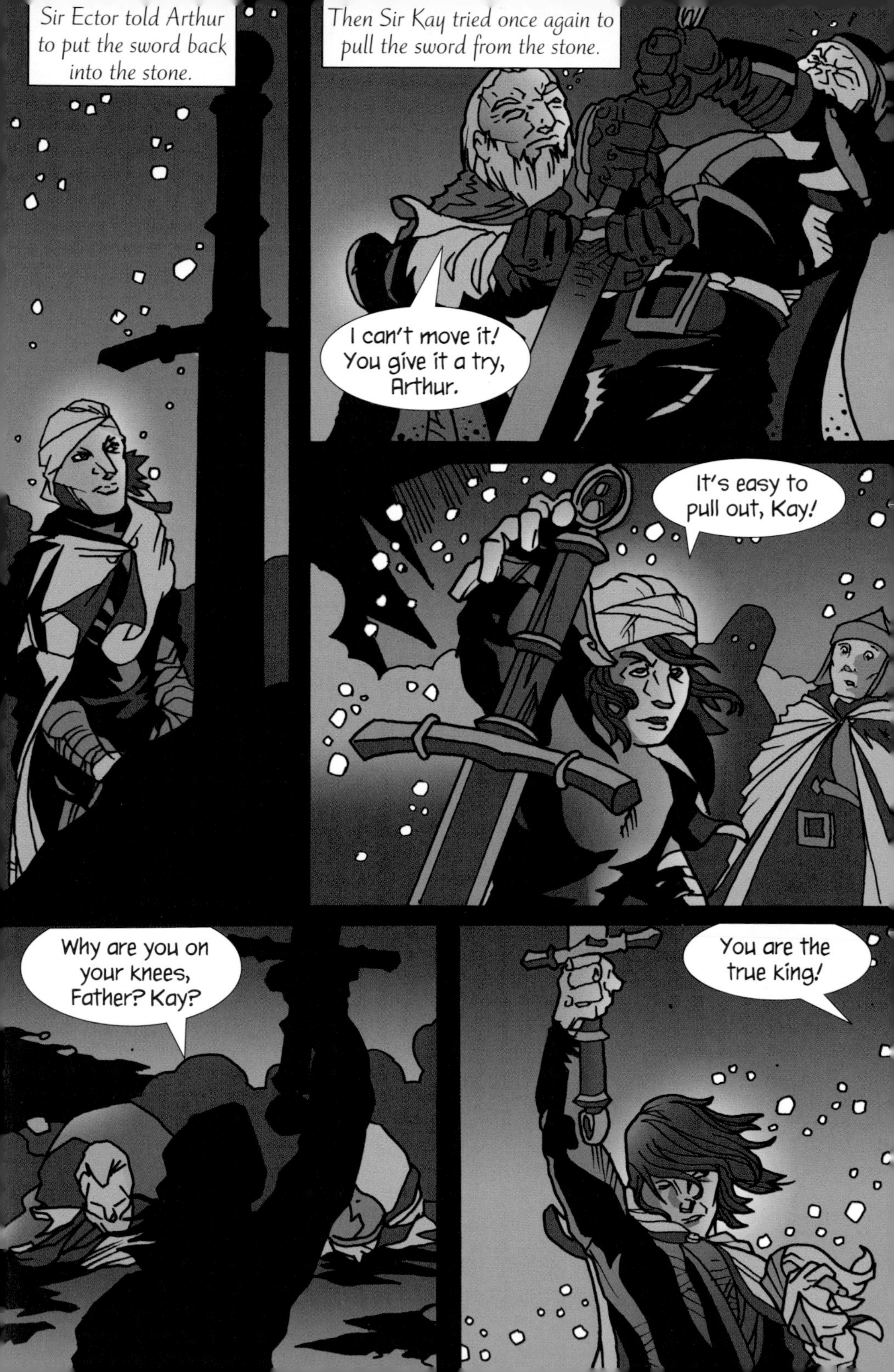
Sir Ector told Arthur to put the sword back into the stone.
Then Sir Kay tried once again to pull the sword from the stone.
I can't move it! You give it a try, Arthur.
It's easy to pull out, Kay!
Why are you on your knees, Father? Kay?
You are the true king!

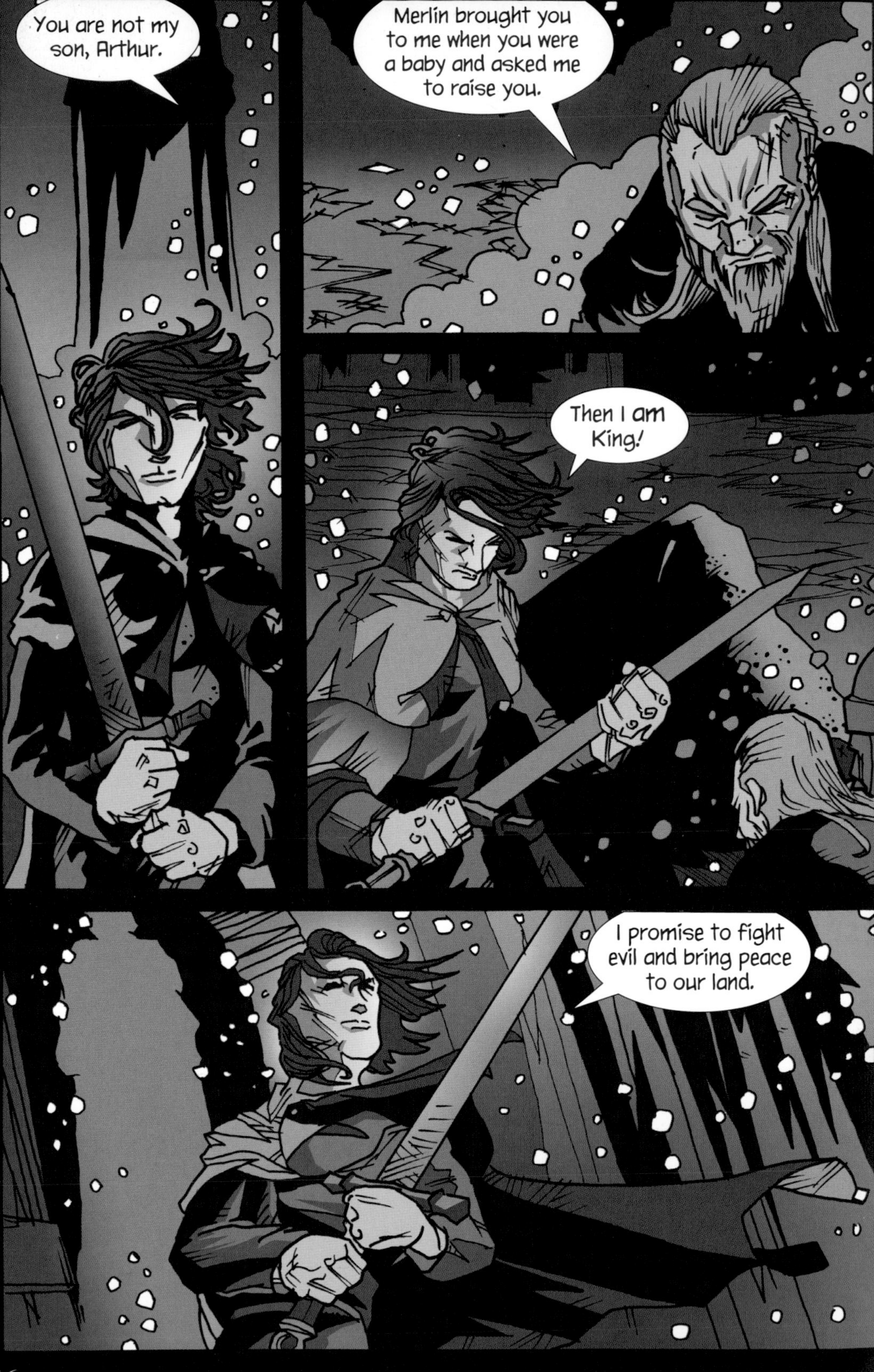
You are not my son, Arthur.
Merlin brought you to me when you were a baby and asked me to raise you.
Then I am King!
I promise to fight evil and bring peace to our land.

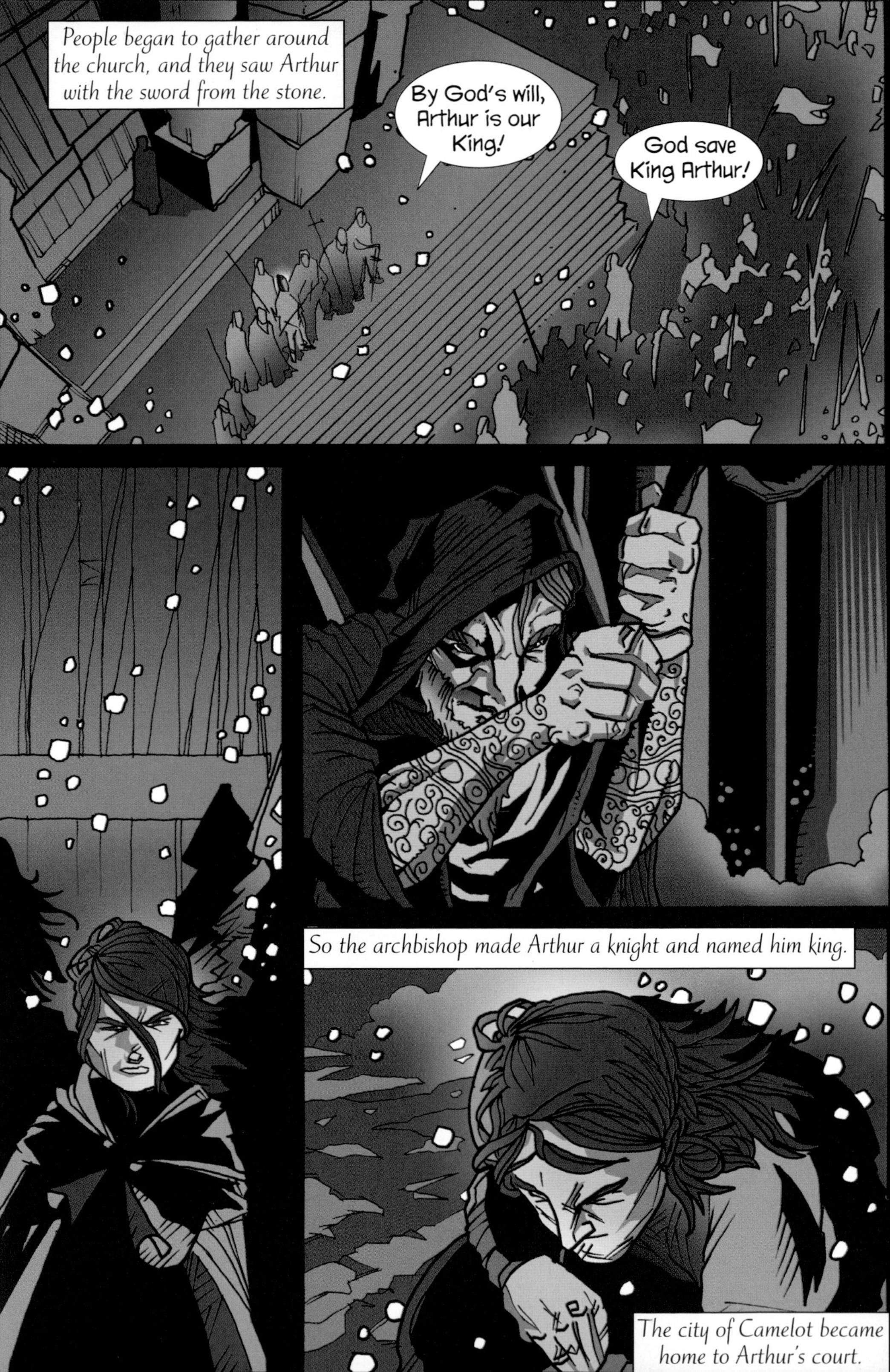
People began to gather around the church, and they saw Arthur with the sword from the stone.
By God's will, Arthur is our King!
God save King Arthur!
So the archbishop made Arthur a knight and named him king.
The city of Camelot became home to Arthur's court.

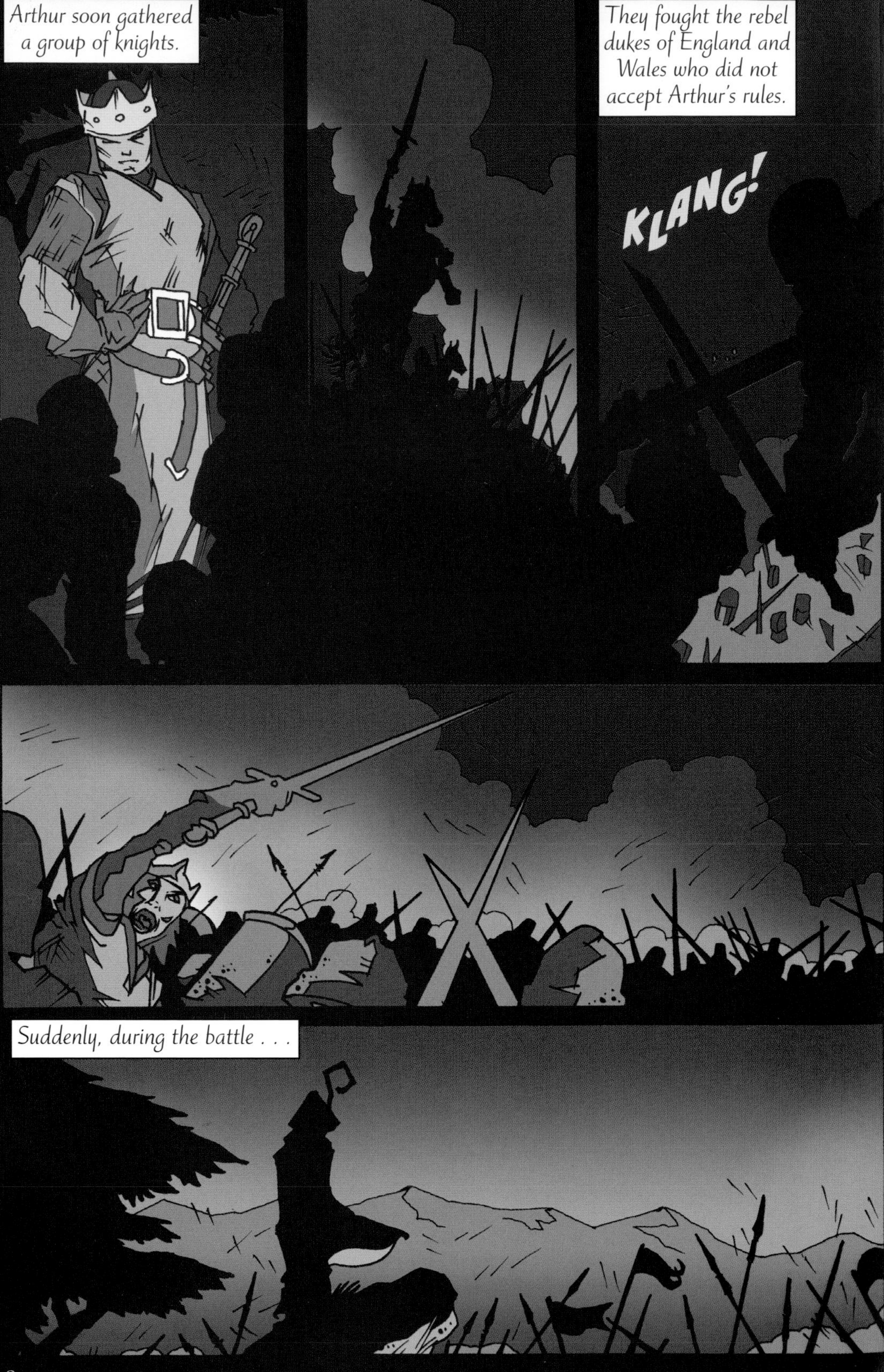
Arthur soon gathered a group of knights.
They fought the rebel dukes of England and Wales who did not accept Arthur's rules.
KLANG!
Suddenly, during the battle . . .

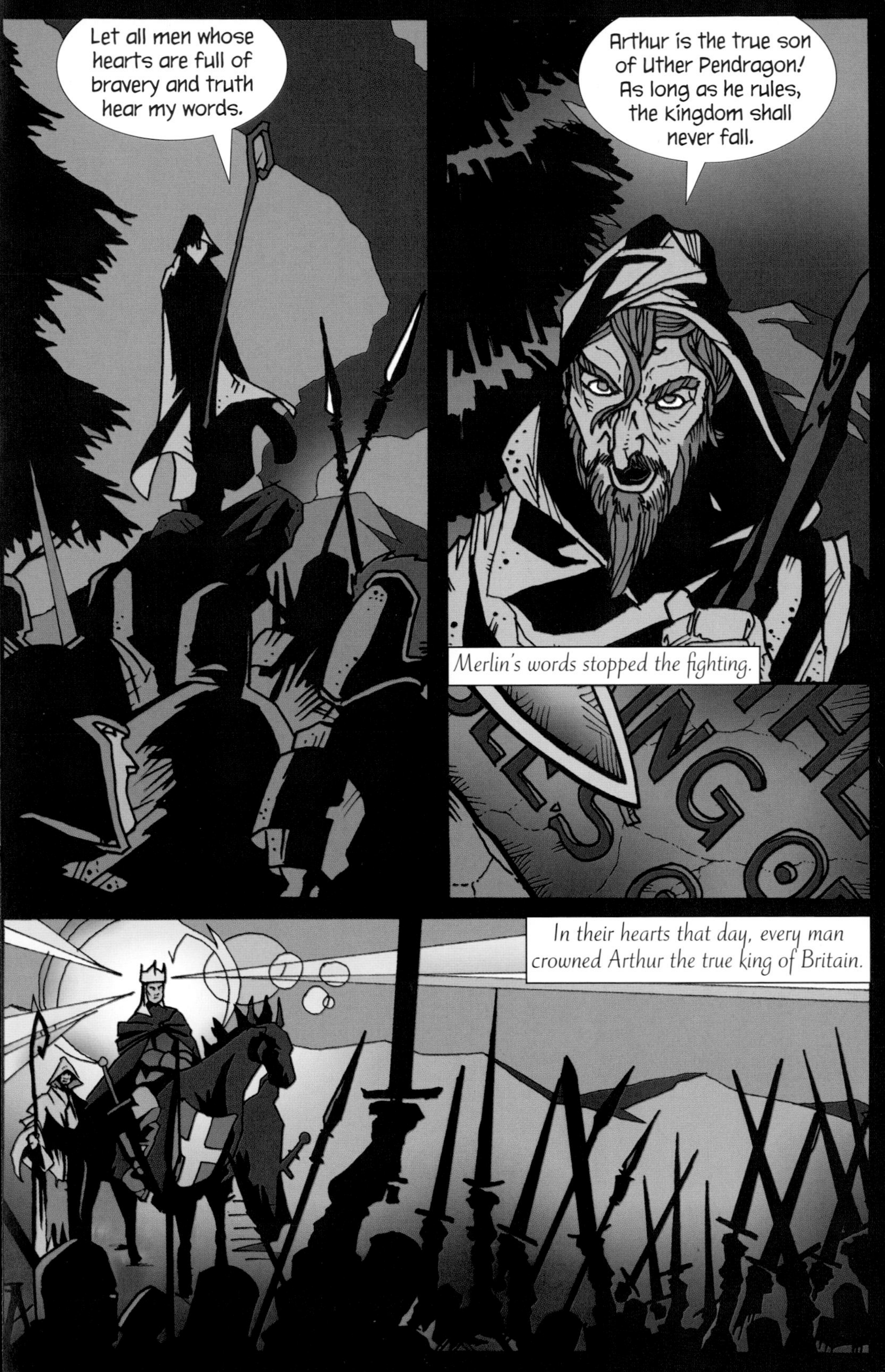
Let all men whose hearts are full of bravery and truth hear my words.
Arthur is the true son of Uther Pendragon! As long as he rules, the kingdom shall never fall.
Merlin's words stopped the fighting.
In their hearts that day, every man crowned Arthur the true king of Britain.

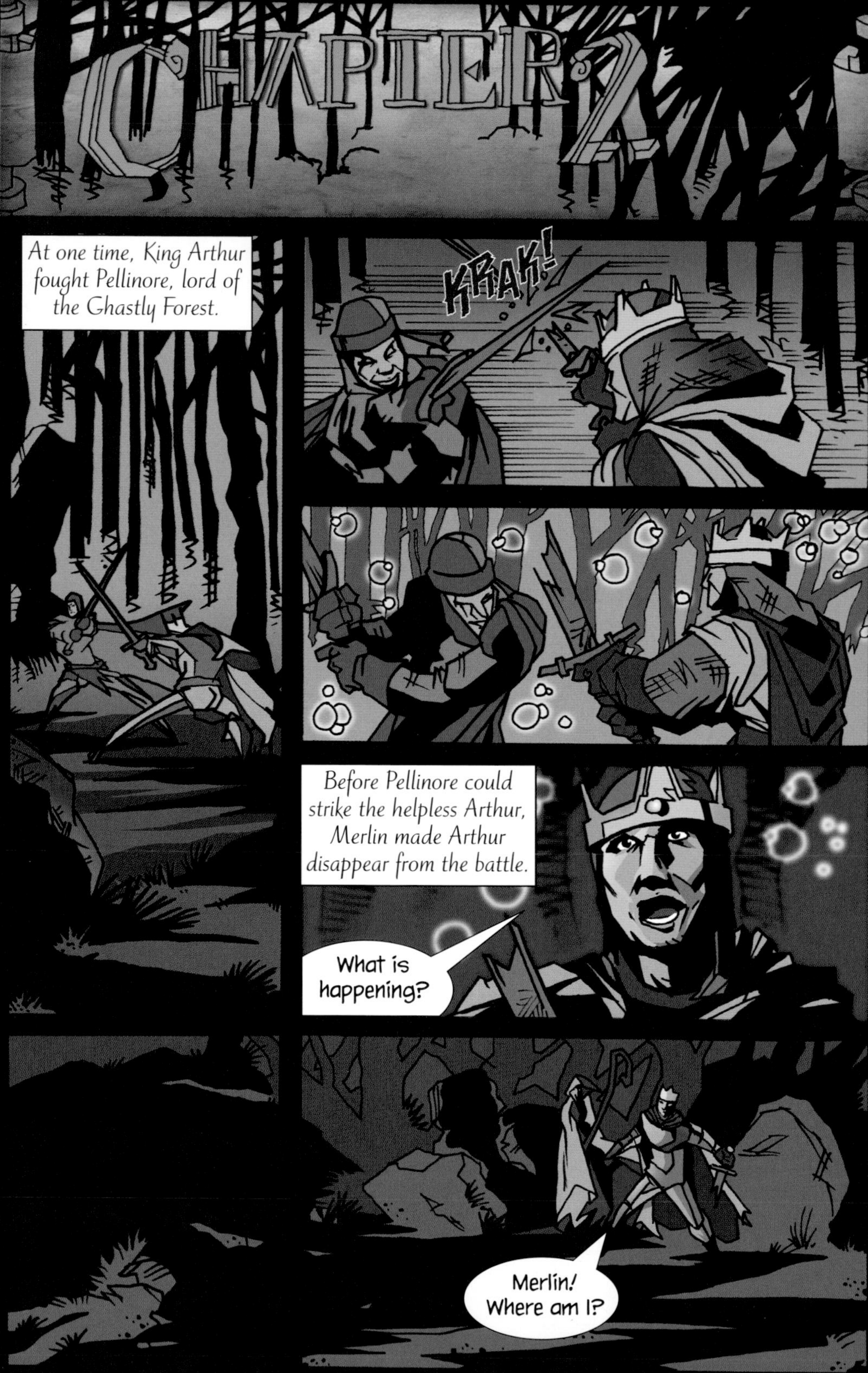
CHAPTER 2
At one time, King Arthur fought Pellinore, lord of the Ghastly Forest.
KRAK!
Before Pellinore could strike the helpless Arthur, Merlin made Arthur disappear from the battle.
What is happening?
Merlin! Where am I?

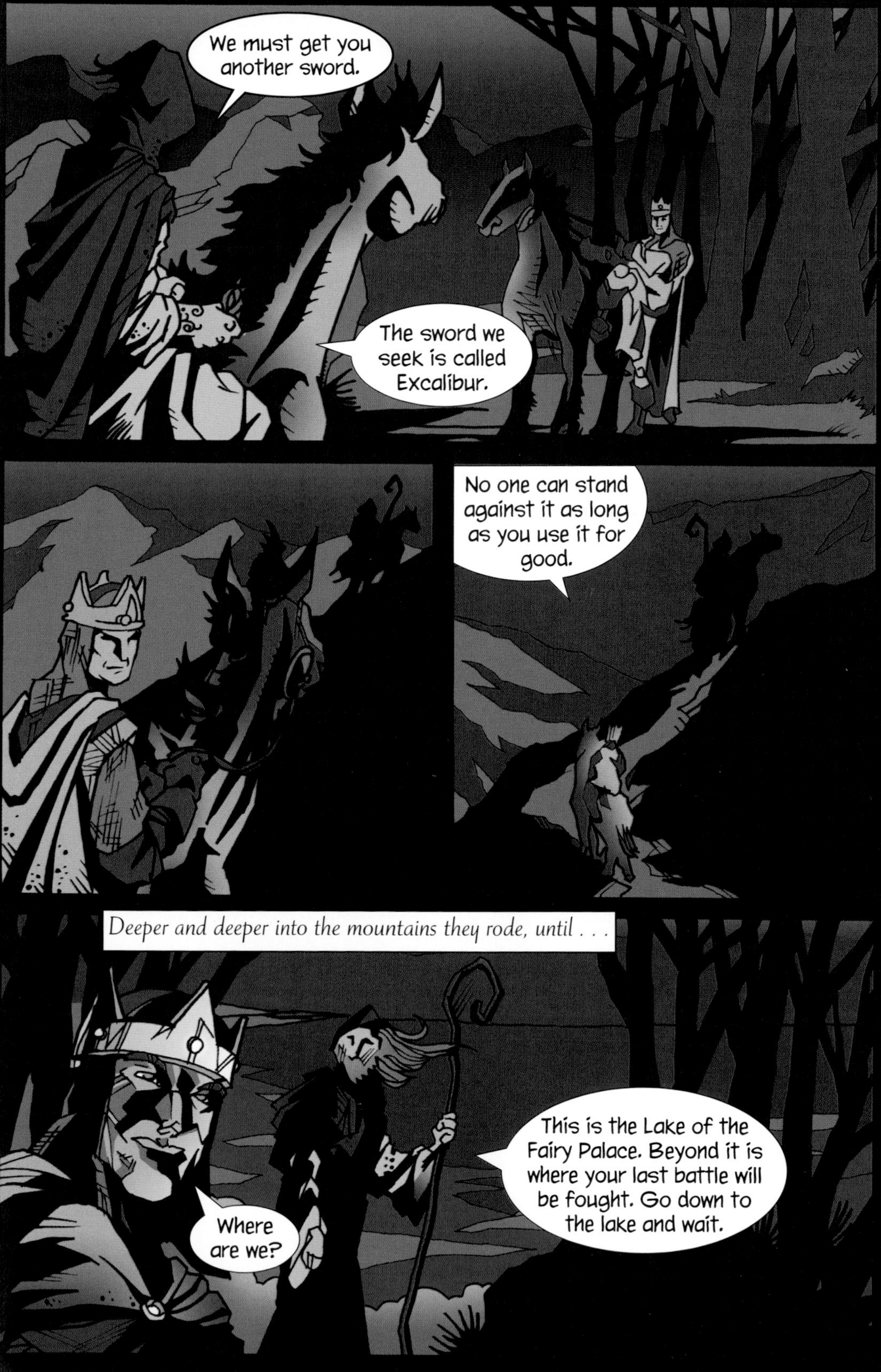
We must get you another sword.
The sword we seek is called Excalibur.
No one can stand against it as long as you use it for good.
Deeper and deeper into the mountains they rode, until . . .
Where are we?
This is the Lake of the Fairy Palace. Beyond it is where your last battle will be fought. Go down to the lake and wait.

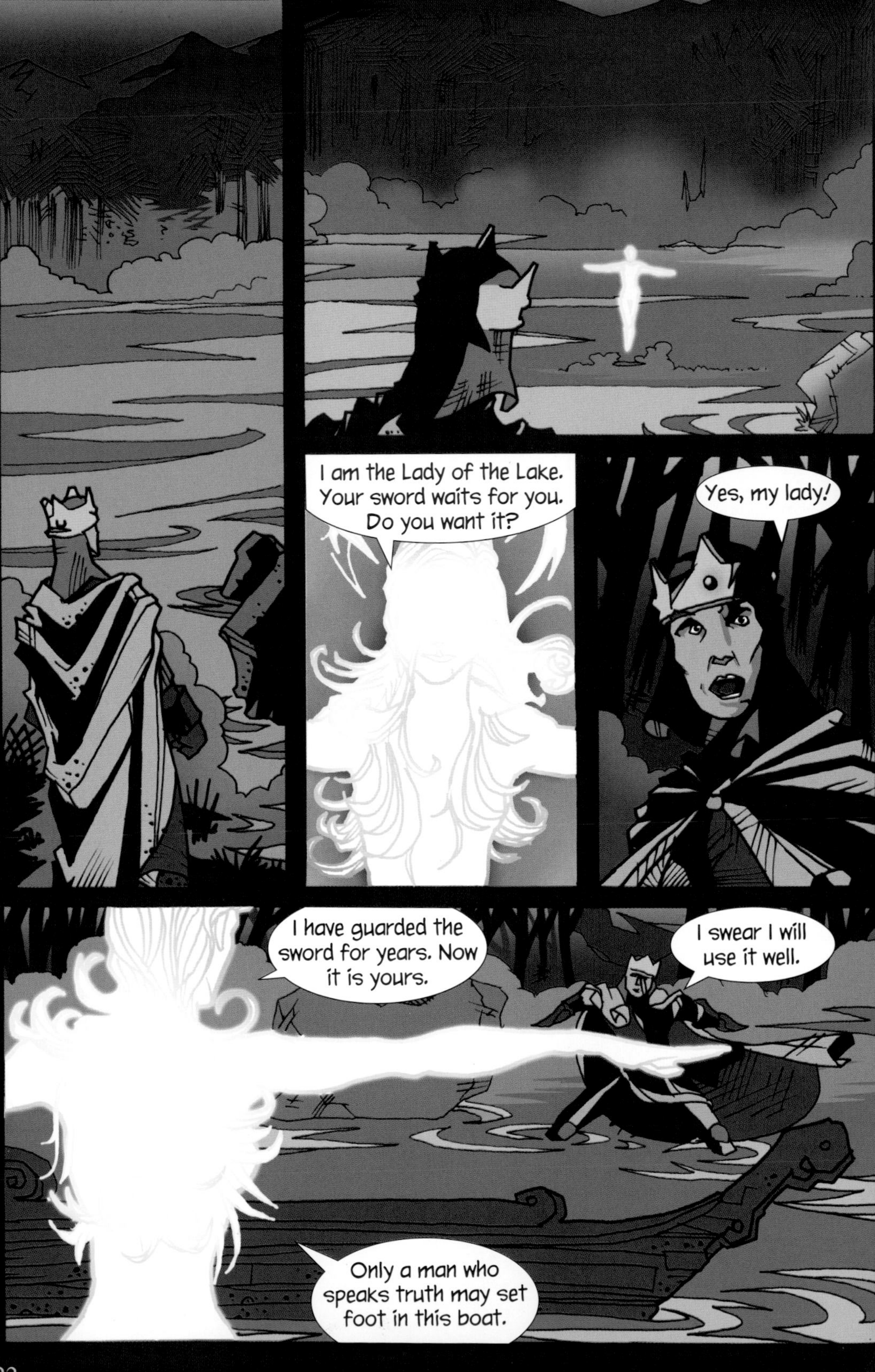
I am the Lady of the Lake. Your sword waits for you. Do you want it?
Yes, my lady!
I have guarded the sword for years. Now it is yours.
I swear I will use it well.
Only a man who speaks truth may set foot in this boat.

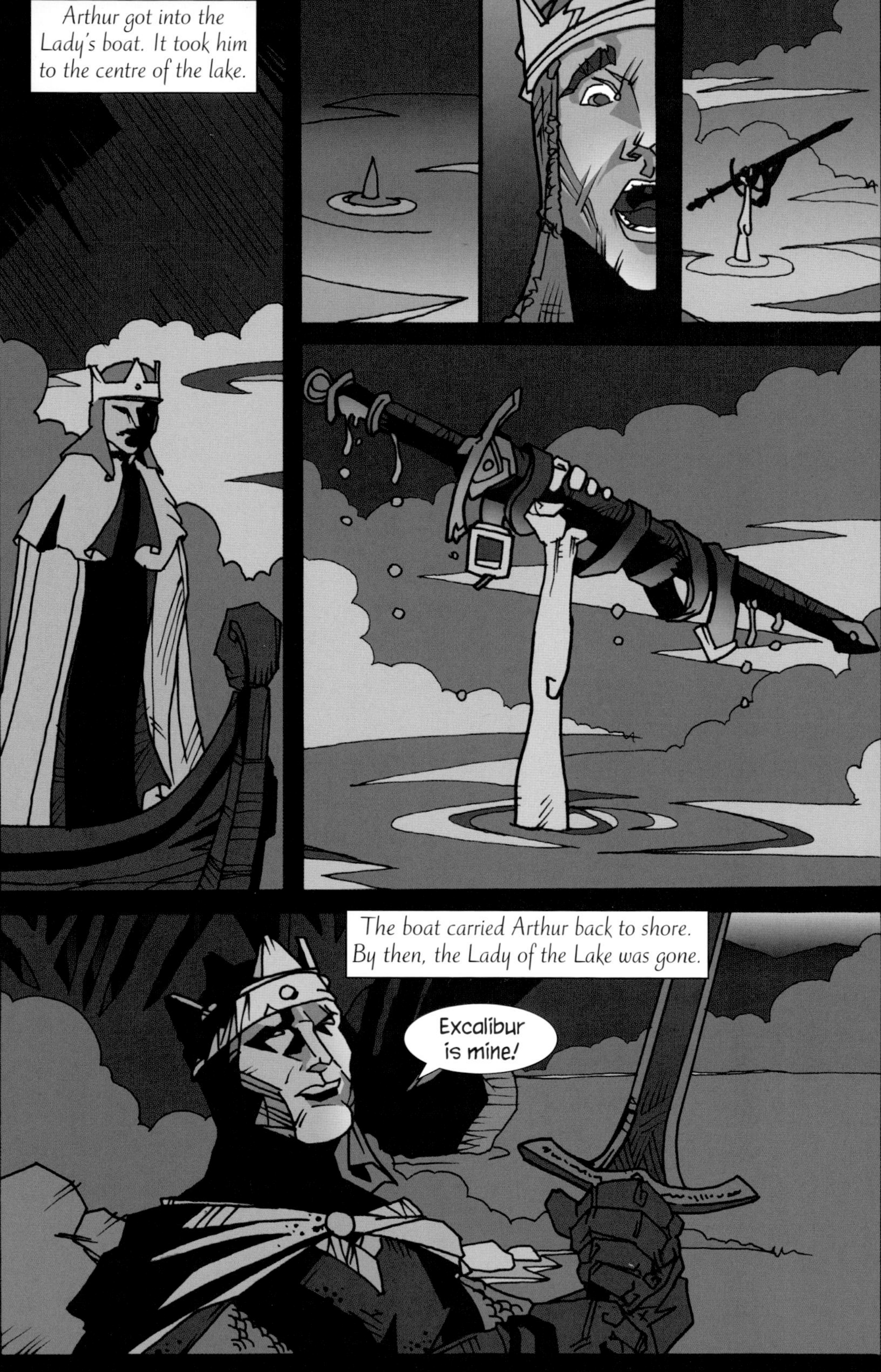
Arthur got into the Lady's boat. It took him to the centre of the lake.
The boat carried Arthur back to shore. By then, the Lady of the Lake was gone.
Excalibur is mine!

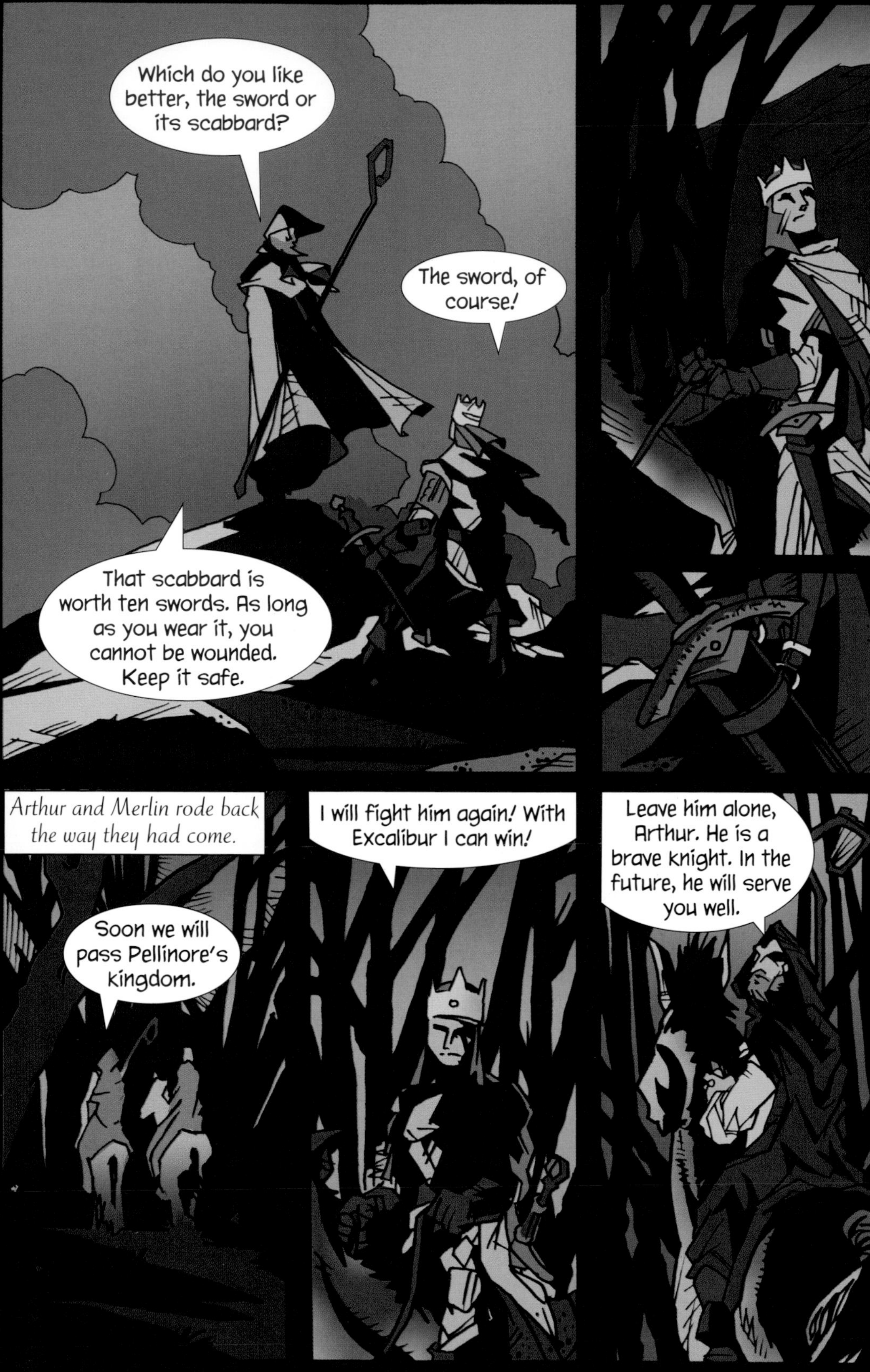

Which do you like better, the sword or its scabbard?
The sword, of course!
That scabbard is worth ten swords. As long as you wear it, you cannot be wounded. Keep it safe.
Arthur and Merlin rode back the way they had come.
Soon we will pass Pellinore's kingdom.
I will fight him again! With Excalibur I can win!
Leave him alone, Arthur. He is a brave knight. In the future, he will serve you well.

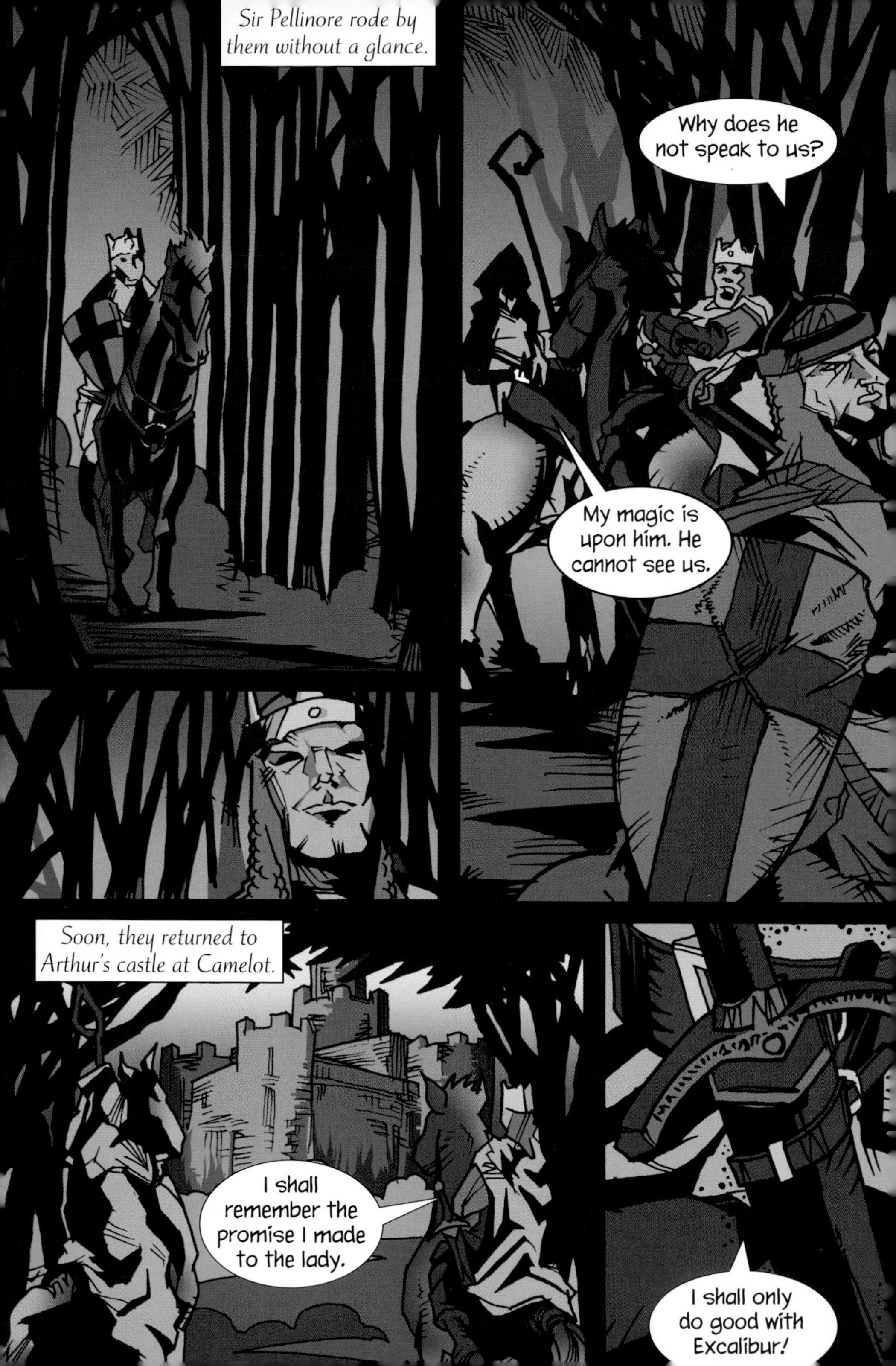
Sir Pellinore rode by them without a glance.
Why does he not speak to us?
My magic is upon him. He cannot see us.
Soon, they returned to Arthur's castle at Camelot.
I shall remember the promise I made to the lady.
I shall only do good with Excalibur!

CHAPTER 3

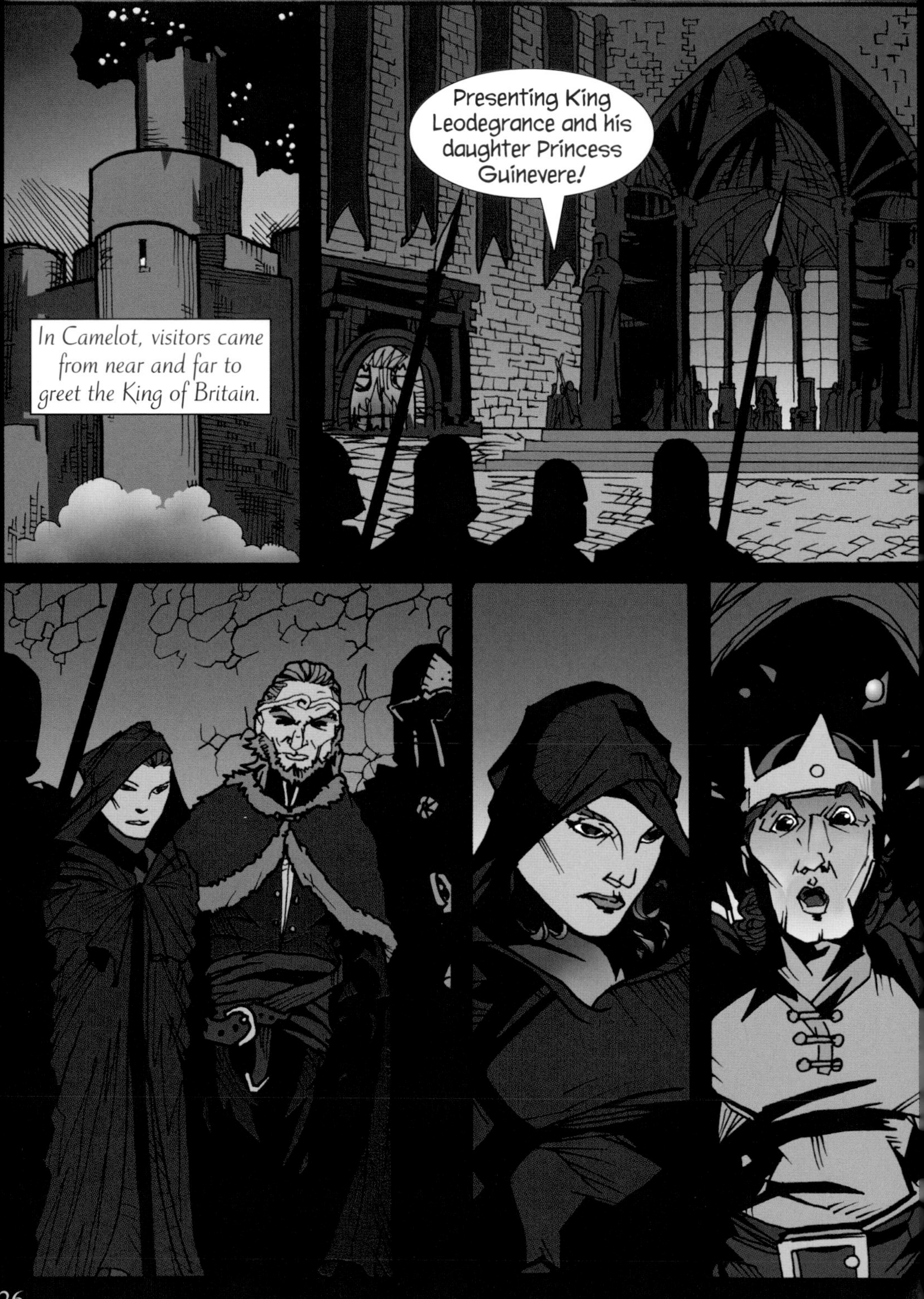
In Camelot, visitors came from near and far to greet the King of Britain.
Presenting King Leodegrance and his daughter Princess Guinevere!

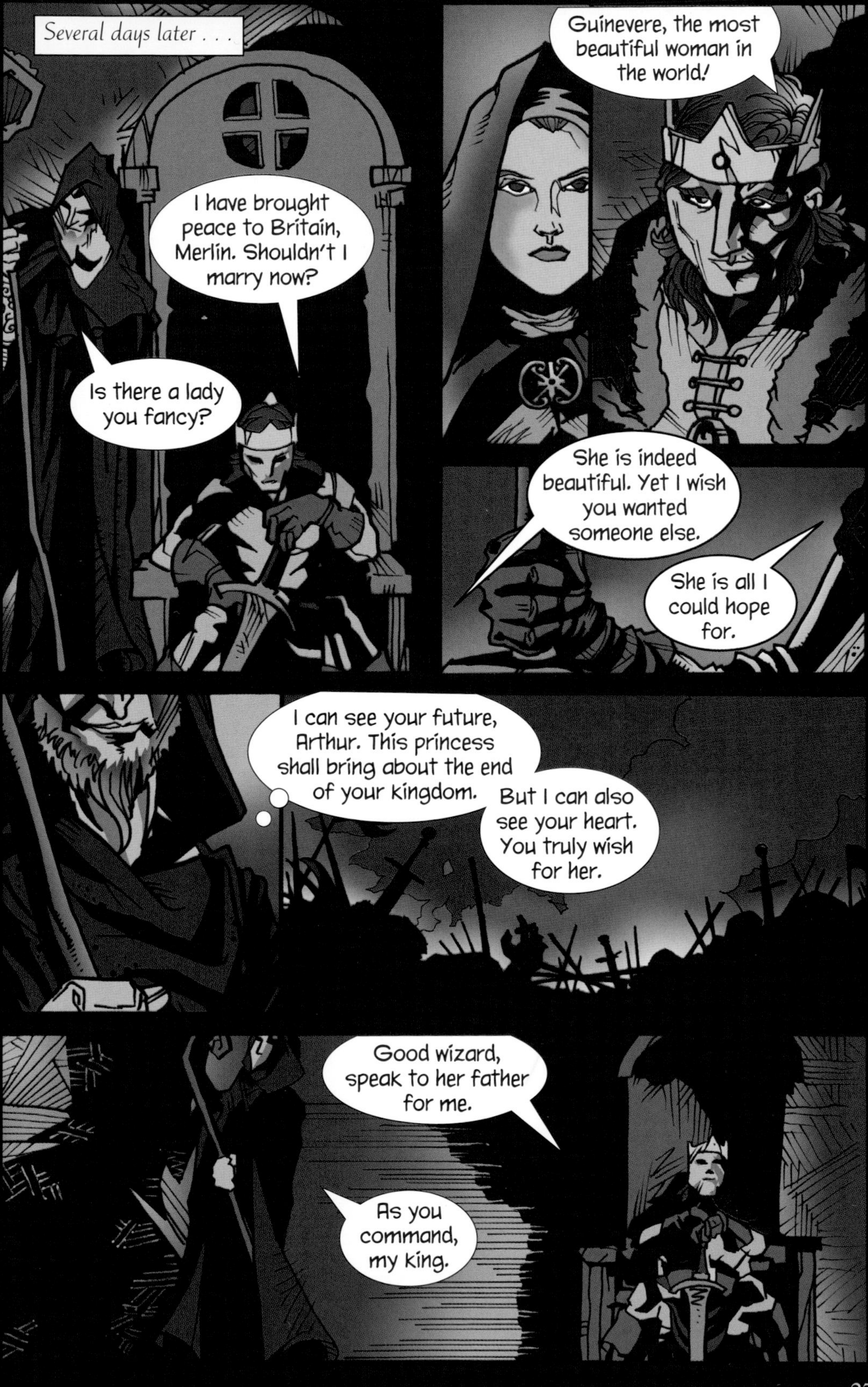
Several days later . . .
I have brought peace to Britain, Merlin. Shouldn't I marry now?
Is there a lady you fancy?
Guinevere, the most beautiful woman in the world!
She is indeed beautiful. Yet I wish you wanted someone else.
She is all I could hope for.
I can see your future, Arthur. This princess shall bring about the end of your kingdom.
But I can also see your heart. You truly wish for her.
Good wizard, speak to her father for me.
As you command, my king.

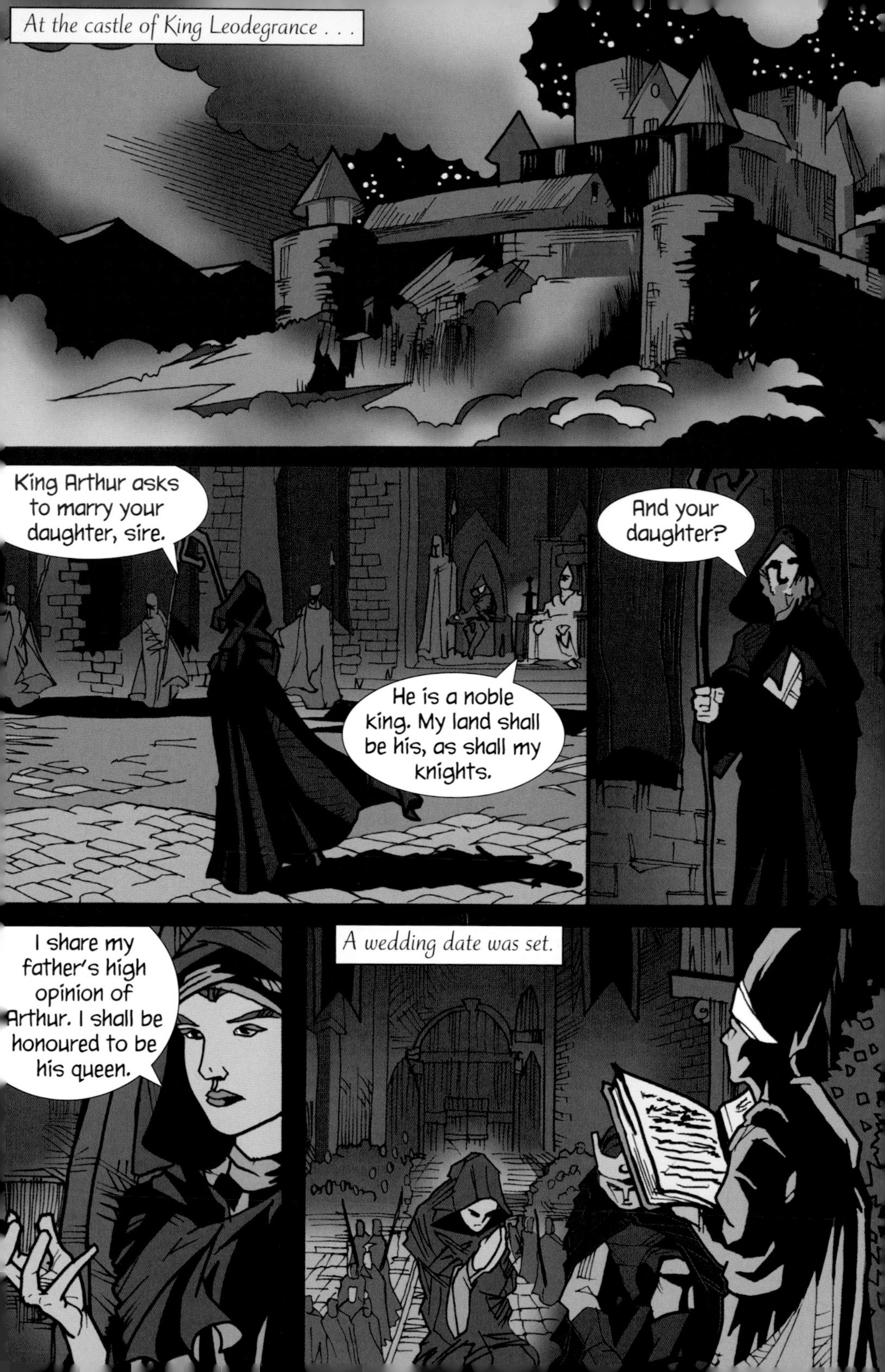
At the castle of King Leodegrance . . .
King Arthur asks to marry your daughter, sire.
He is a noble king. My land shall be his, as shall my knights.
And your daughter?
I share my father's high opinion of Arthur. I shall be honoured to be his queen.
A wedding date was set.

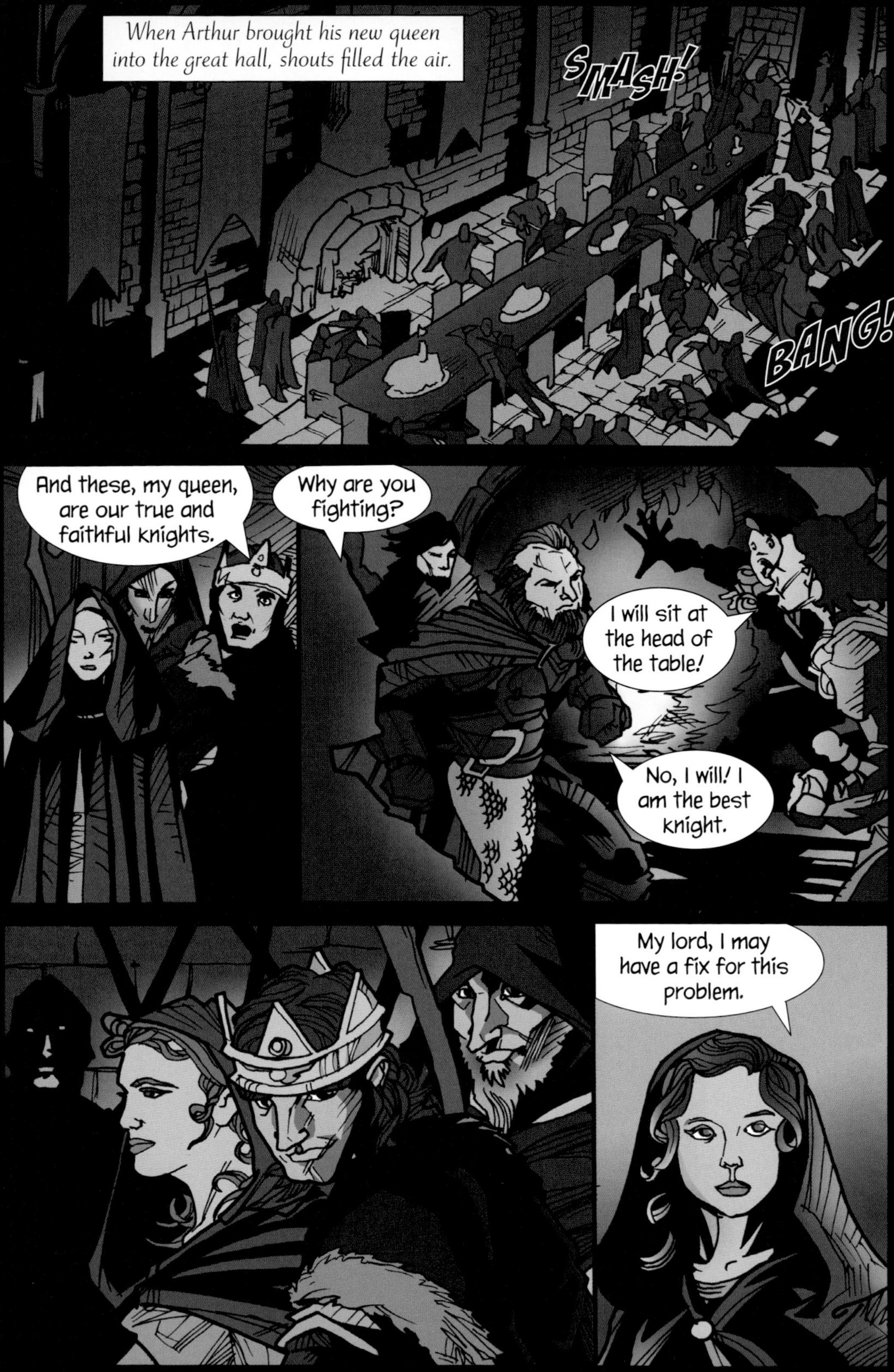
When Arthur brought his new queen into the great hall, shouts filled the air.
SMASH!
BANG!
And these, my queen, are our true and faithful knights.
Why are you fighting?
I will sit at the head of the table!
No, I will! I am the best knight.
My lord, I may have a fix for this problem.

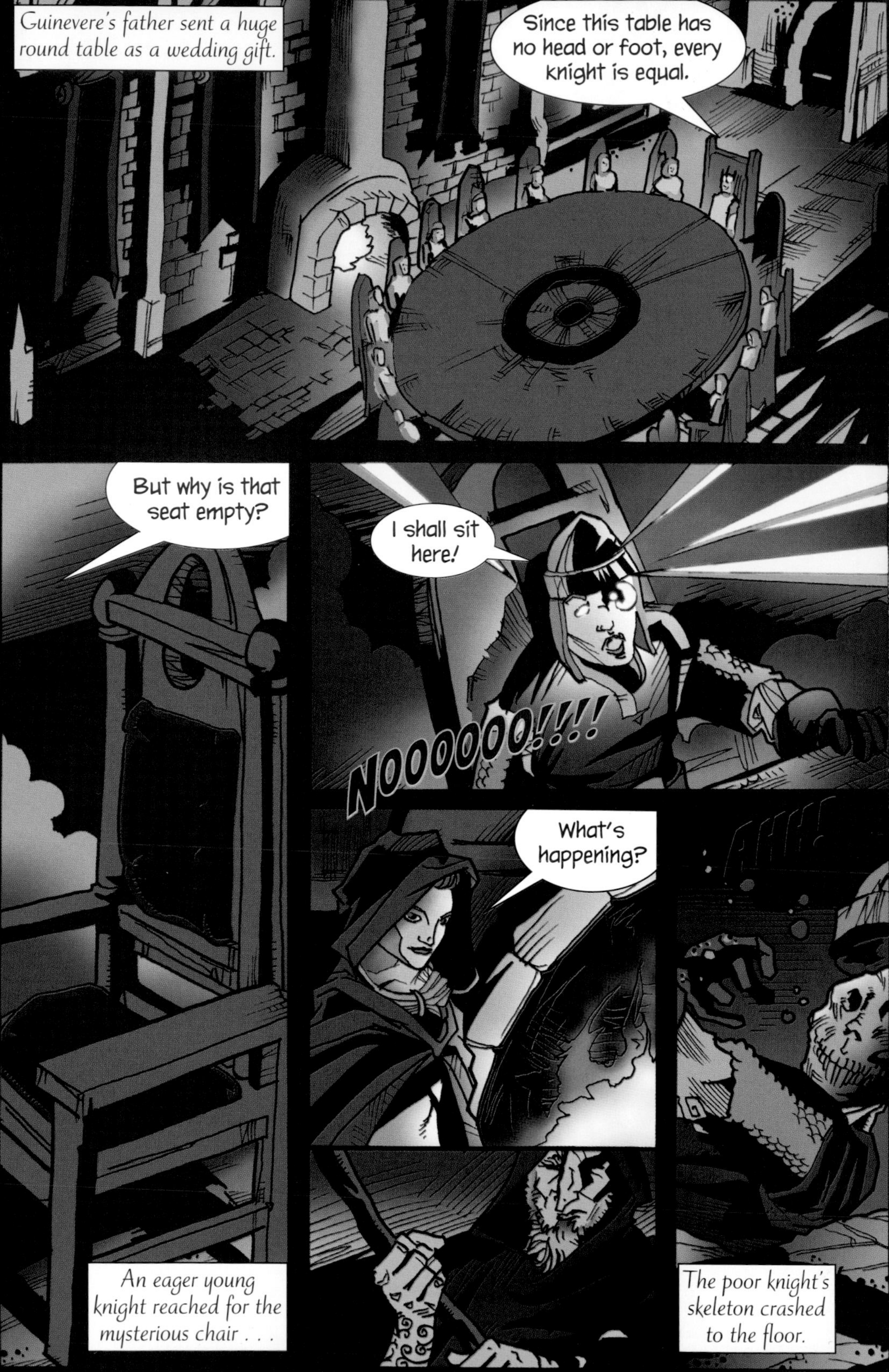

Guinevere's father sent a huge round table as a wedding gift.
Since this table has no head or foot, every knight is equal.
But why is that seat empty?
I shall sit here!
NOOOOOO!!!!
What's happening?
An eager young knight reached for the mysterious chair . . .
The poor knight's skeleton crashed to the floor.

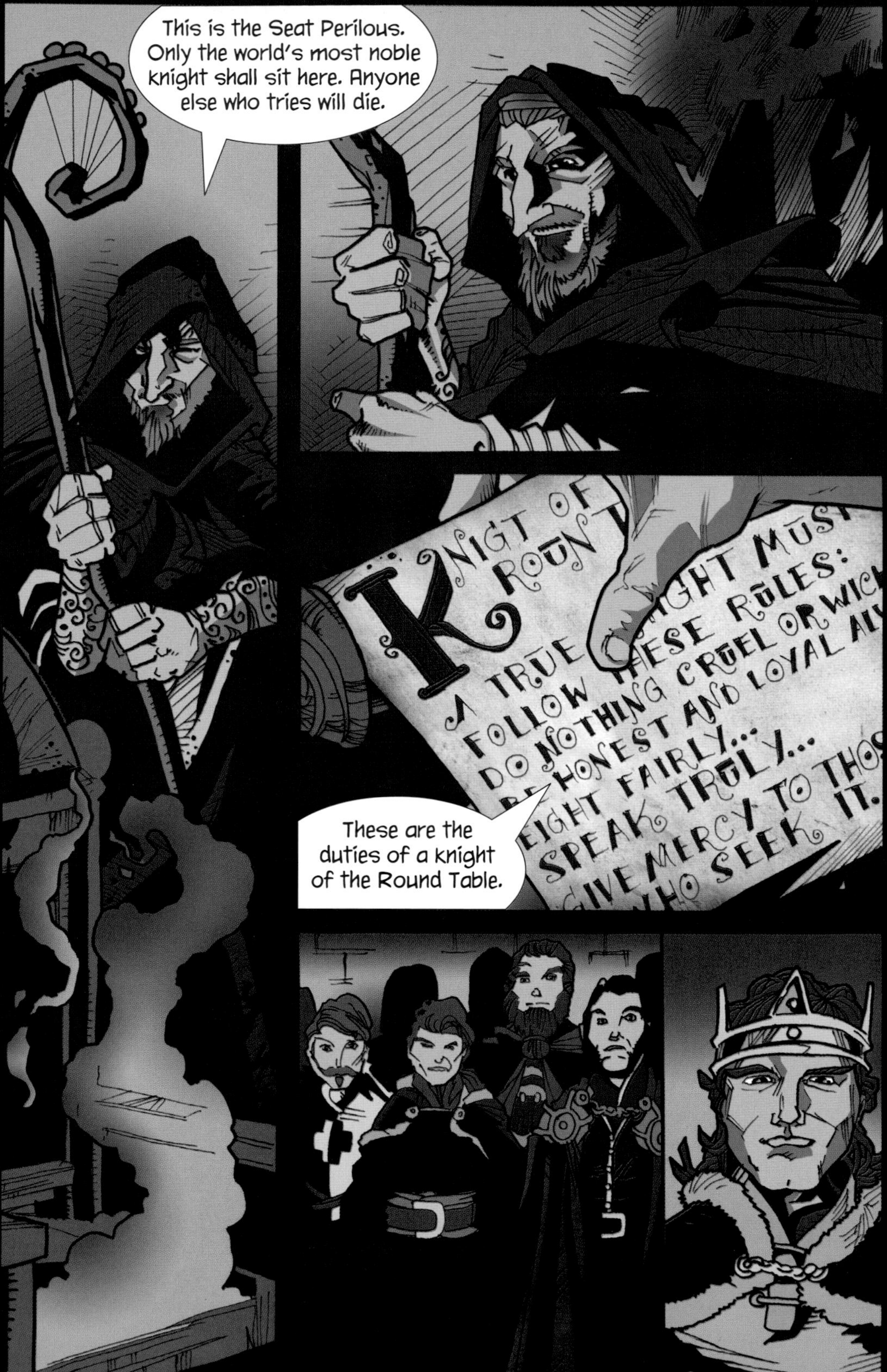
This is the Seat Perilous. Only the world's most noble knight shall sit here. Anyone else who tries will die.
These are the duties of a knight of the Round Table.

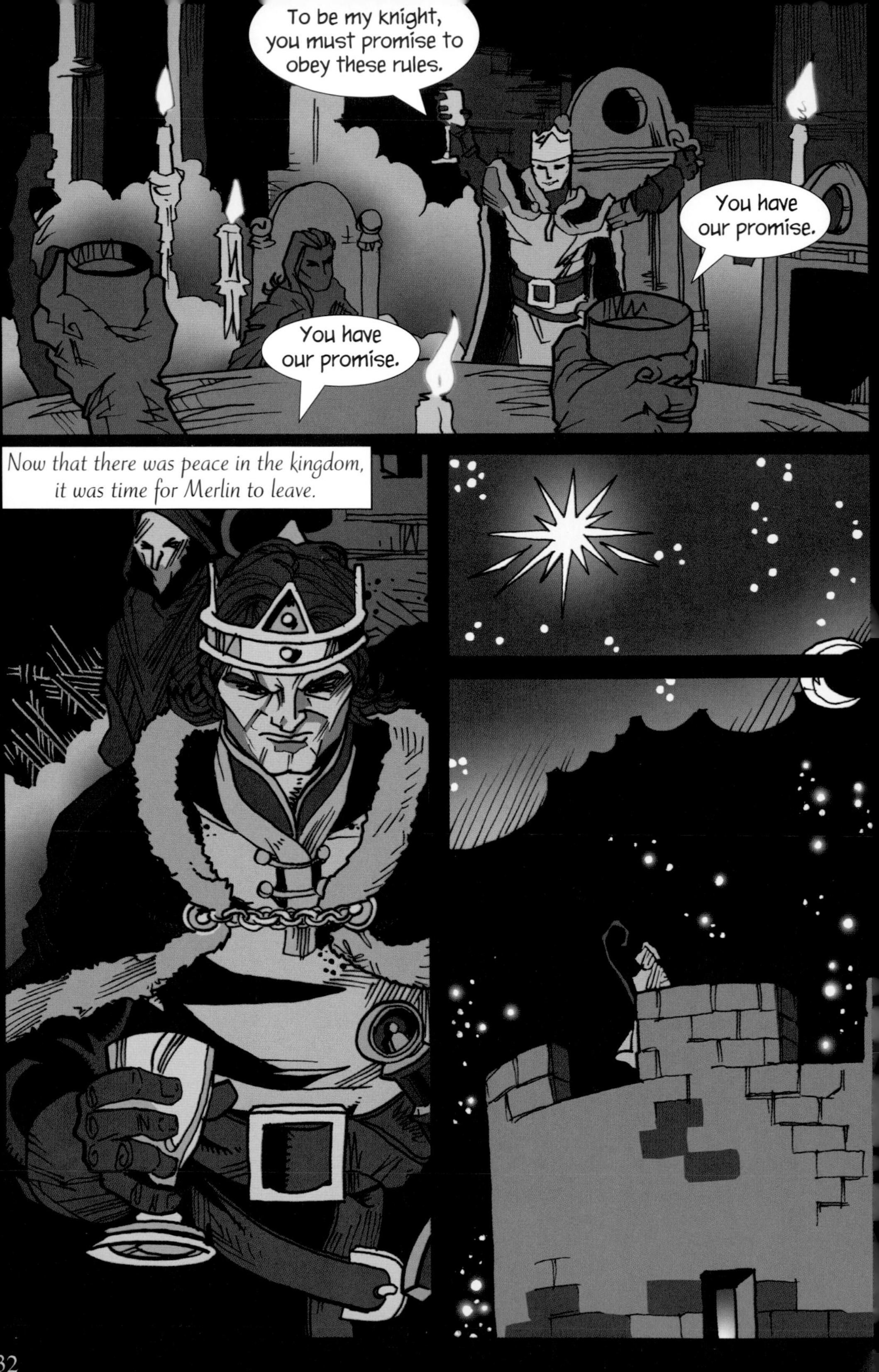
To be my knight, you must promise to obey these rules.
You have our promise.
You have our promise.
Now that there was peace in the kingdom, it was time for Merlin to leave.

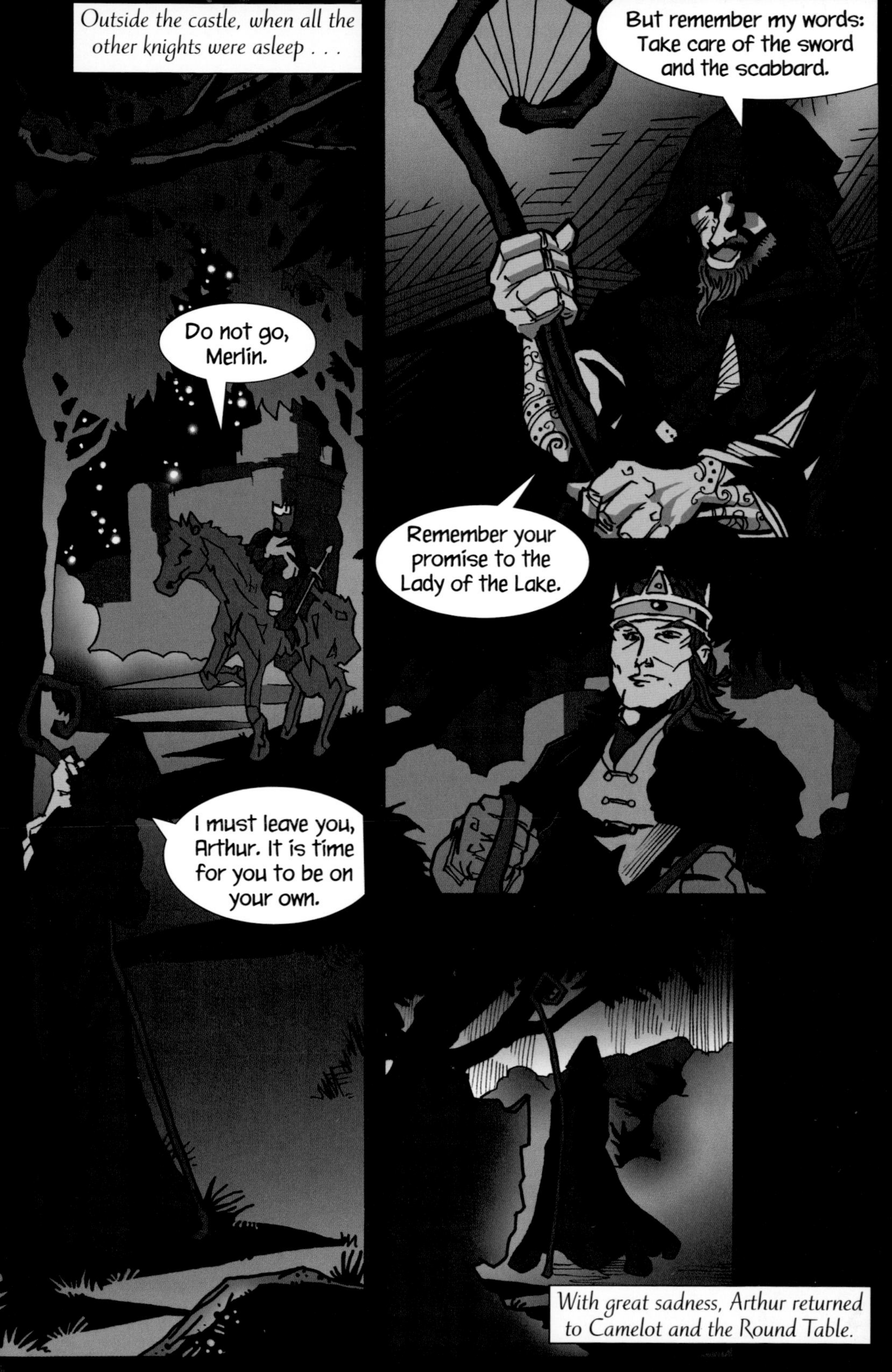
Outside the castle, when all the other knights were asleep . . .
Do not go, Merlin.
I must leave you, Arthur. It is time for you to be on your own.
But remember my words: Take care of the sword and the scabbard.
Remember your promise to the Lady of the Lake.
With great sadness, Arthur returned to Camelot and the Round Table.

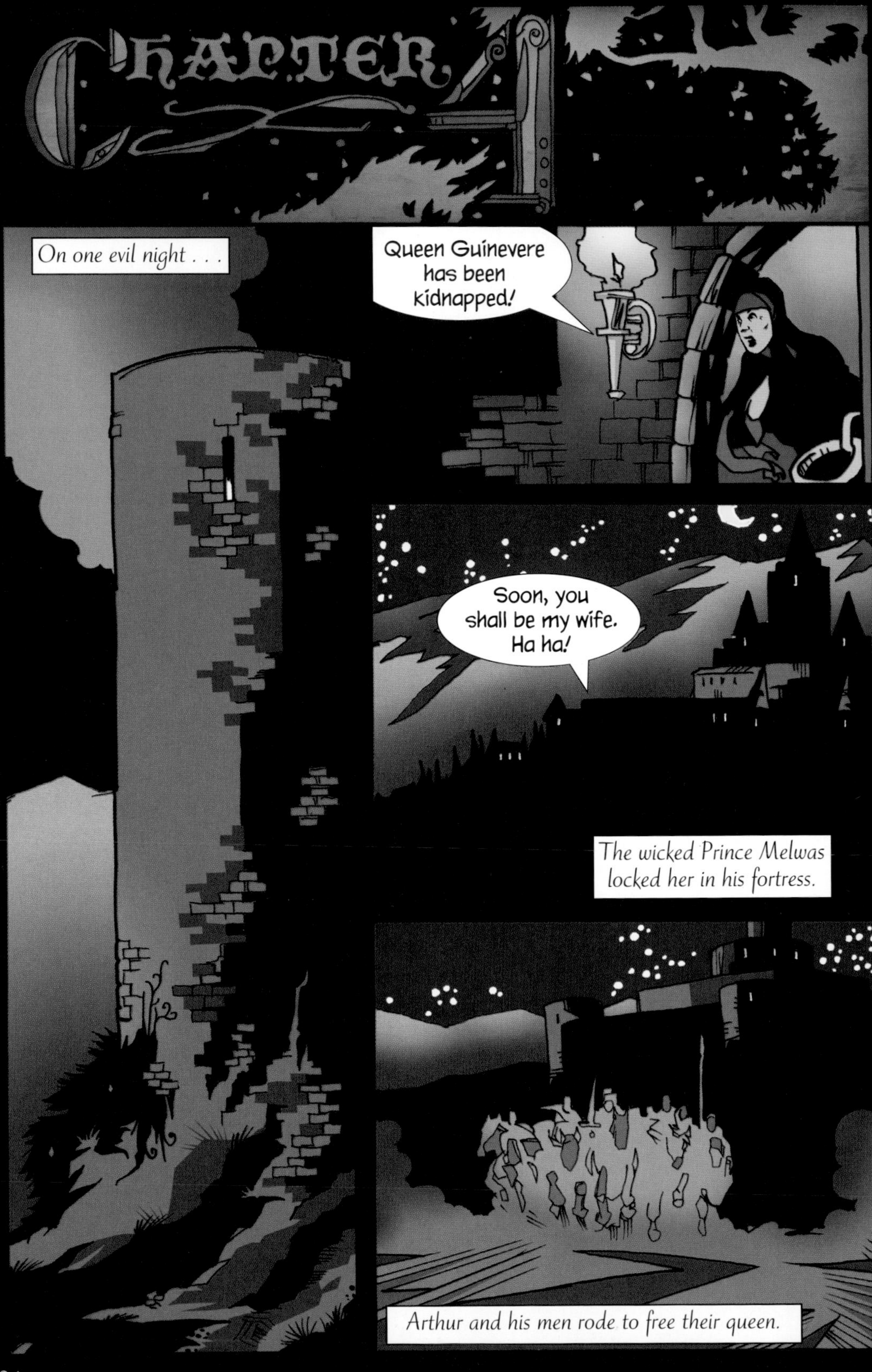
CHAPTER
On one evil night . . .
Queen Guinevere has been kidnapped!
Soon, you shall be my wife. Ha ha!
The wicked Prince Melwas locked her in his fortress.
Arthur and his men rode to free their queen.

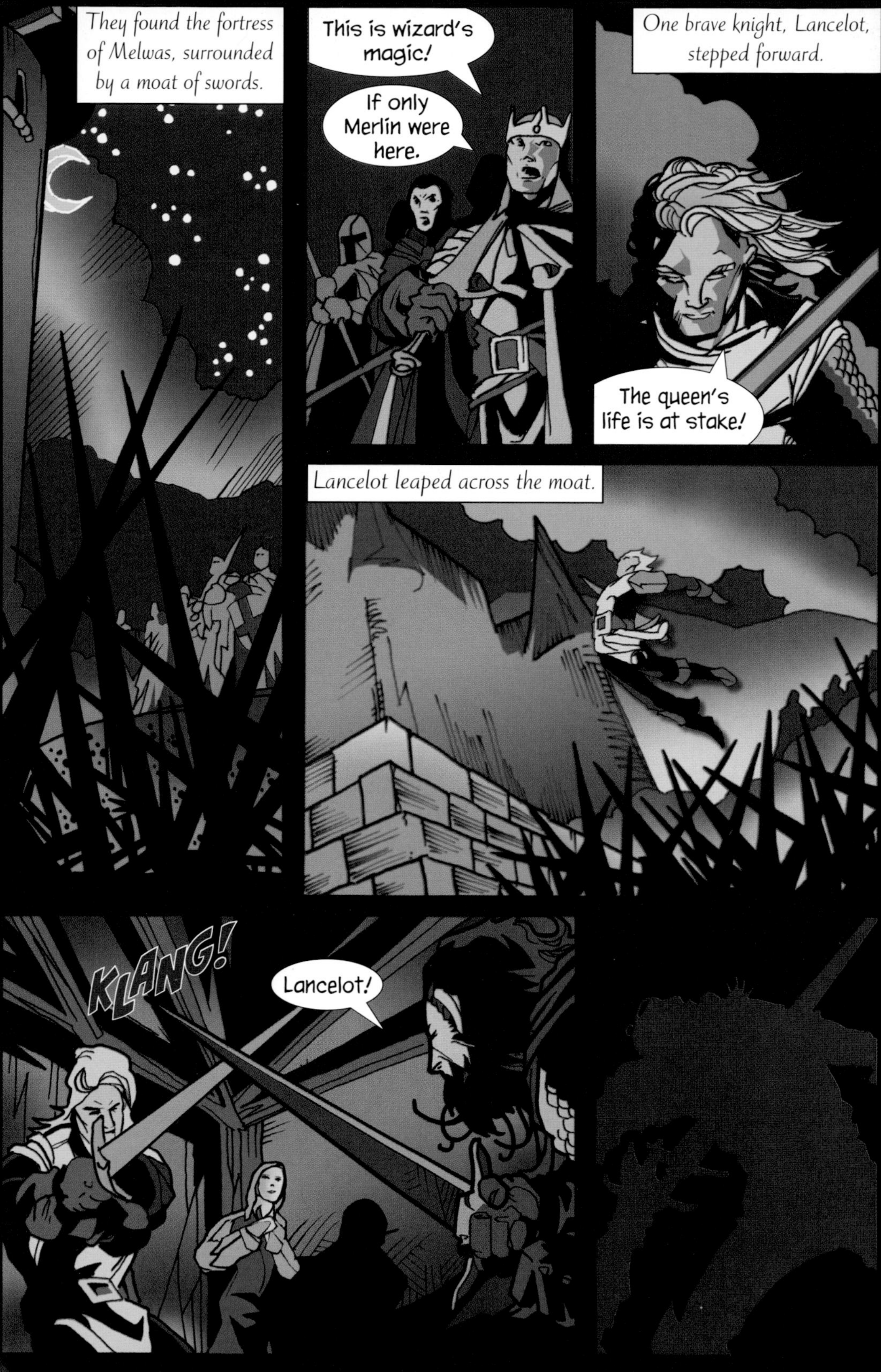
They found the fortress of Melwas, surrounded by a moat of swords.
This is wizard's magic!
If only Merlin were here.
One brave knight, Lancelot, stepped forward.
The queen's life is at stake!
Lancelot leaped across the moat.
KLANG!
Lancelot!

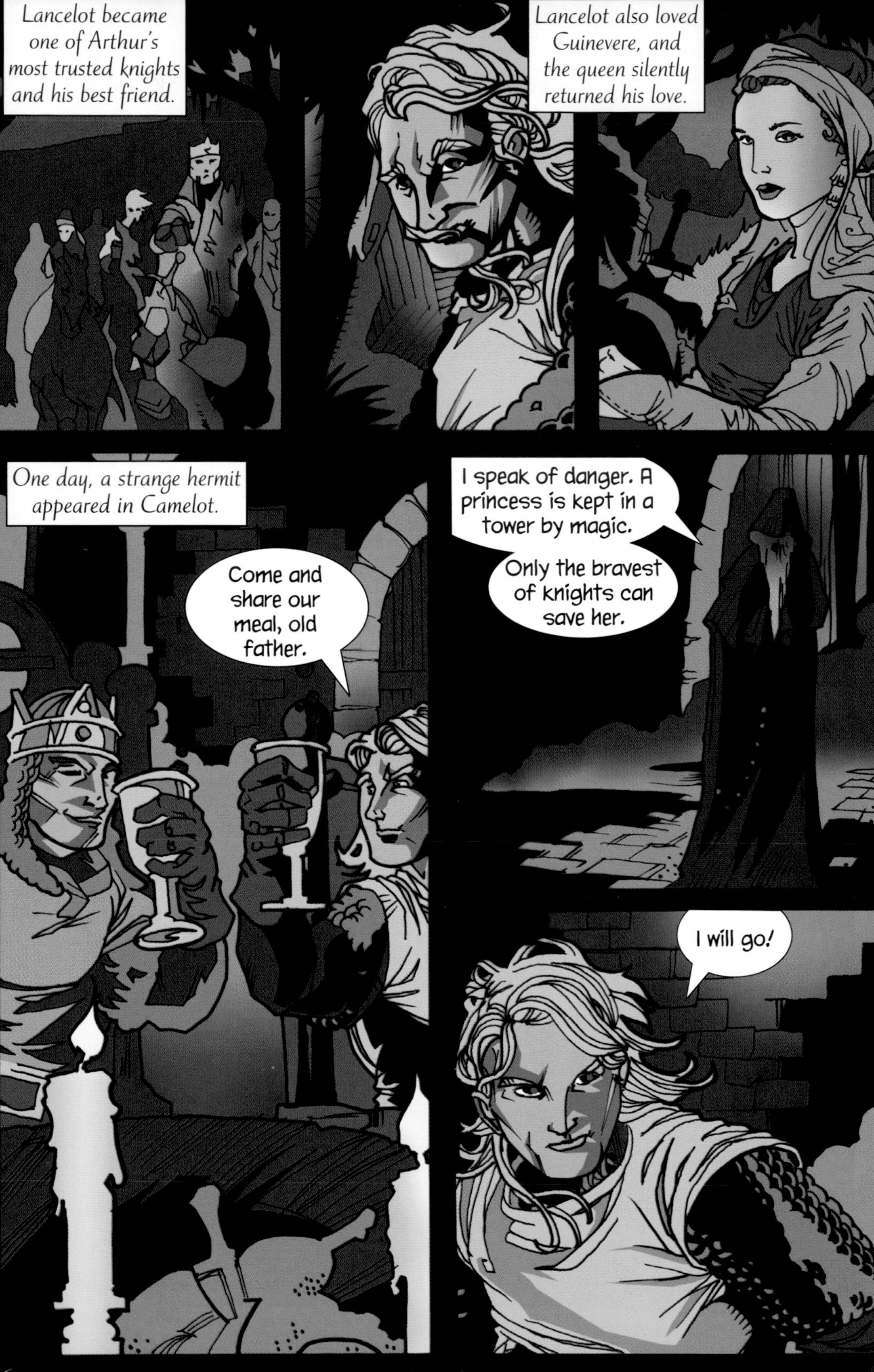
Lancelot became one of Arthur's most trusted knights and his best friend.
Lancelot also loved Guinevere, and the queen silently returned his love.
One day, a strange hermit appeared in Camelot.
Come and share our meal, old father.
I speak of danger. A princess is kept in a tower by magic.
Only the bravest of knights can save her.
I will go!

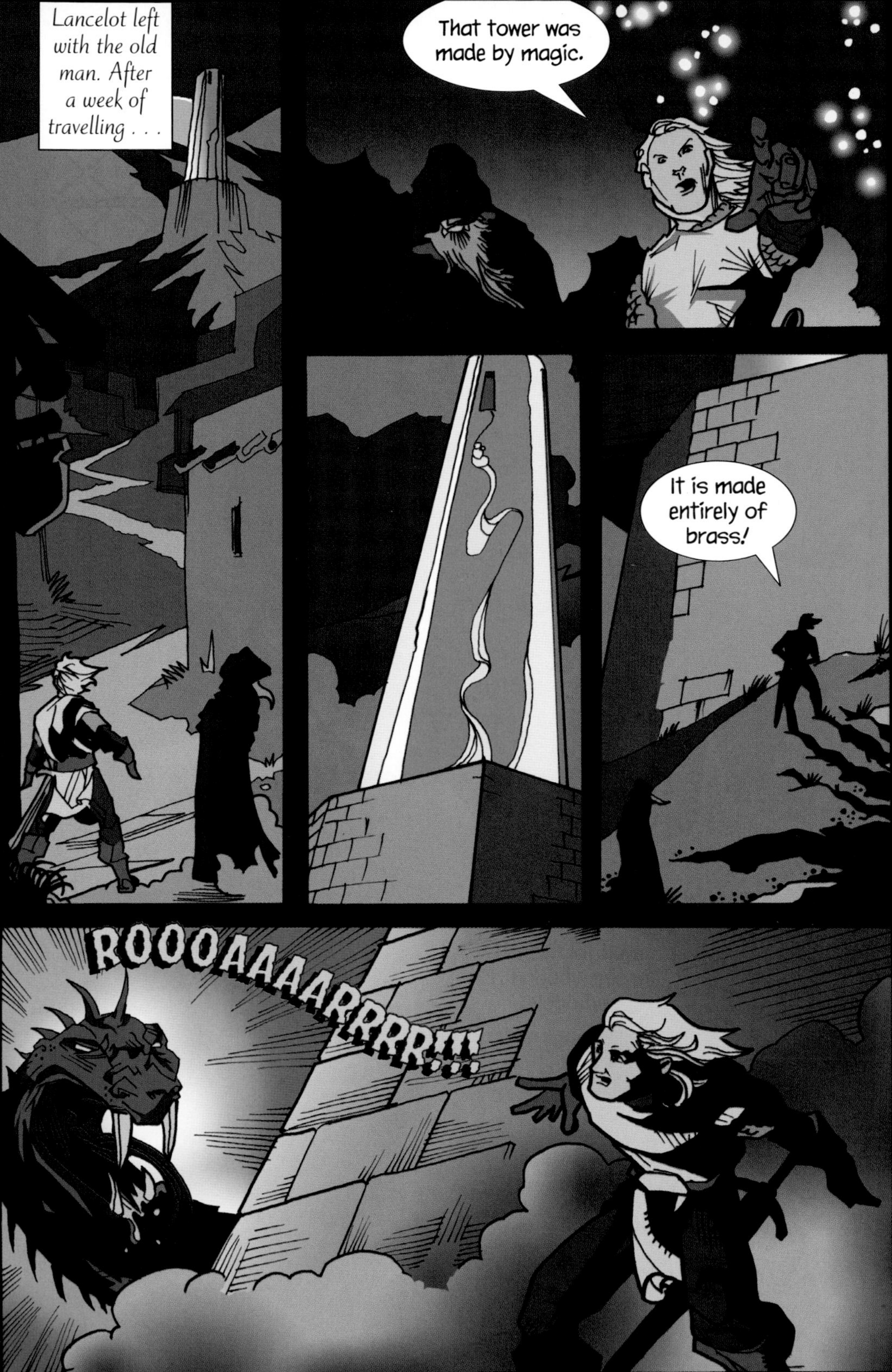
Lancelot left with the old man. After a week of travelling . . .
That tower was made by magic.
It is made entirely of brass!
ROOOAAAAARRRR!!!

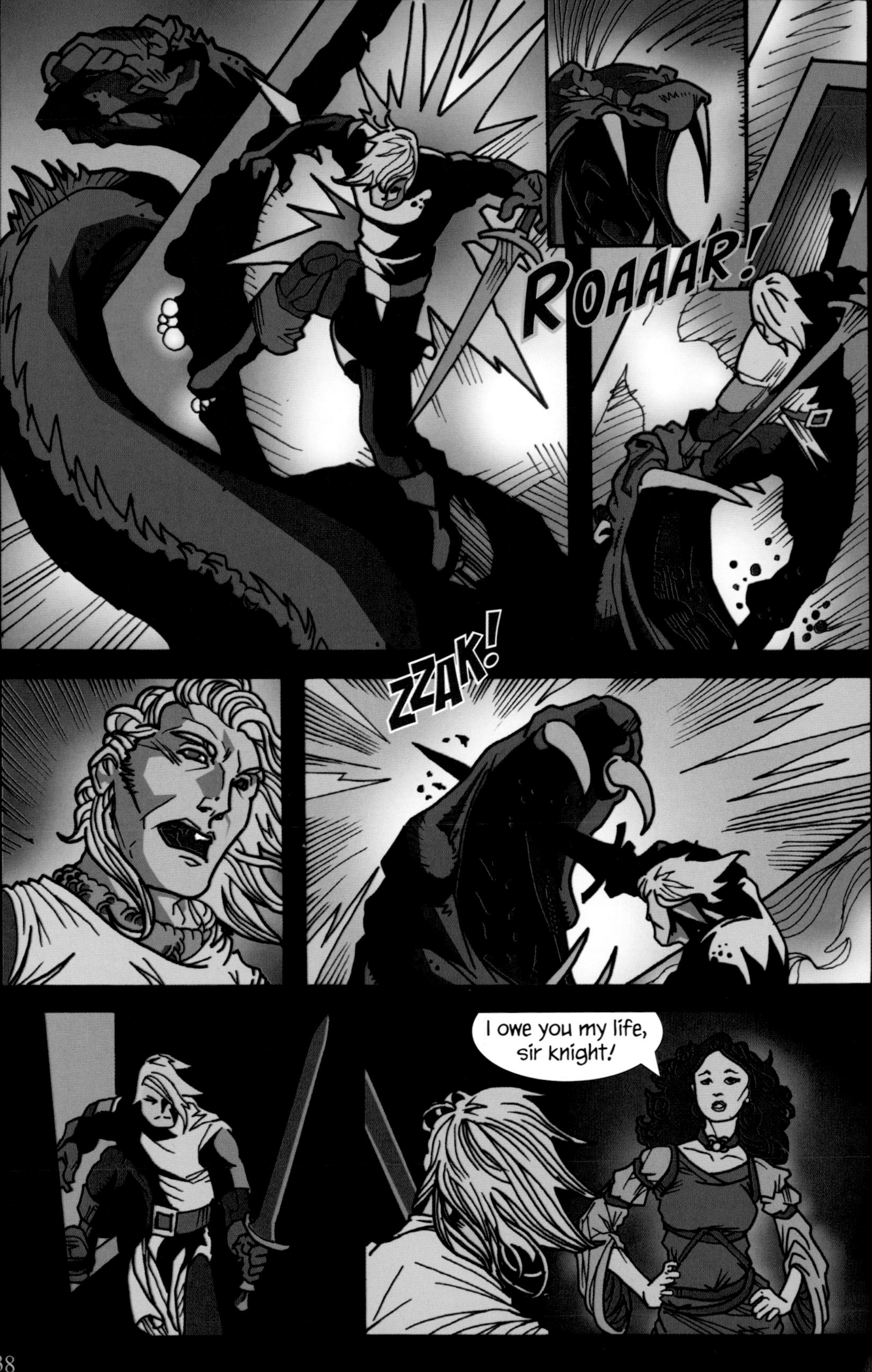
ROAAAR!
ZZAK!
I owe you my life, sir knight!

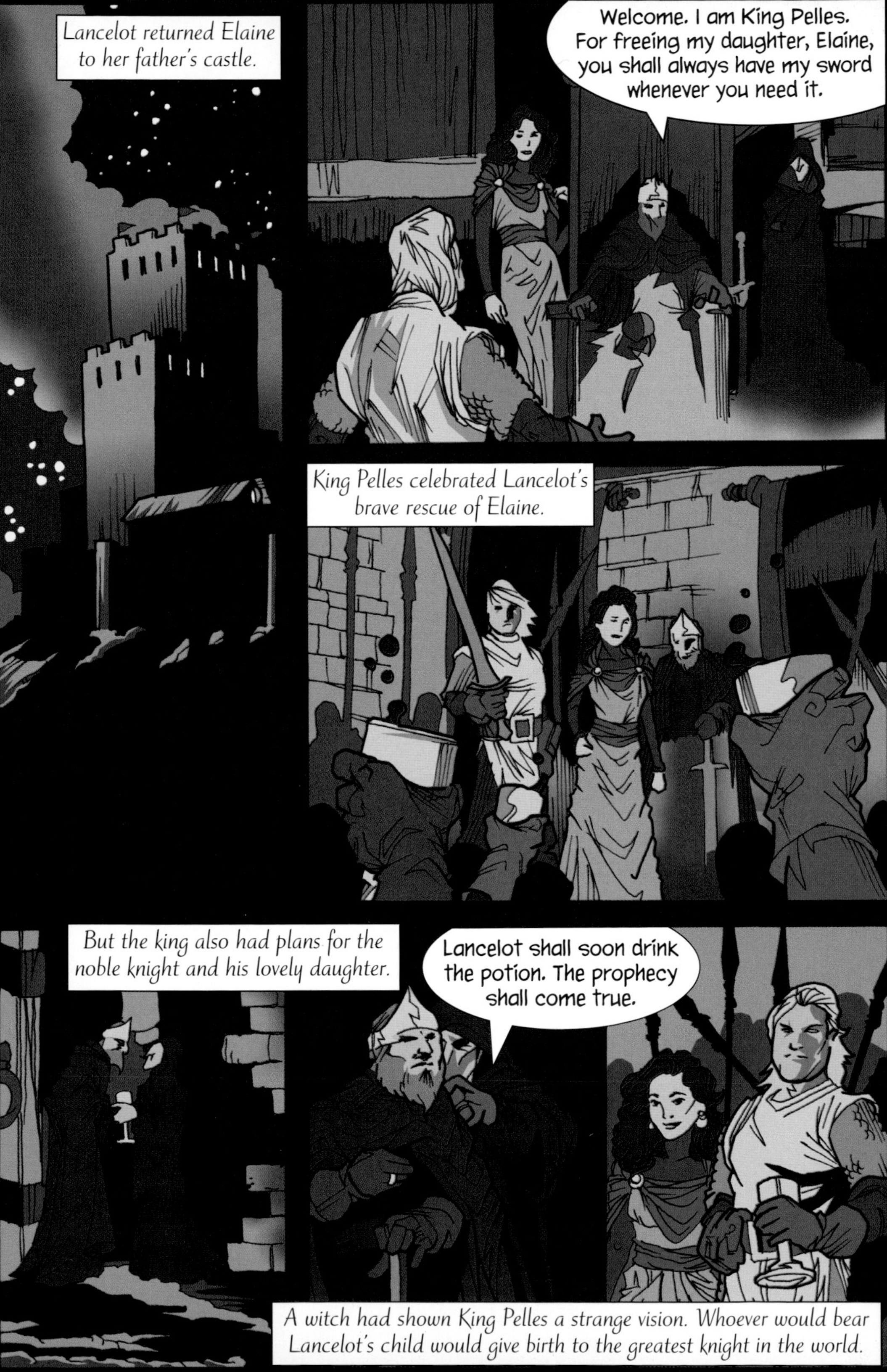
Lancelot returned Elaine to her father's castle.
Welcome. I am King Pelles. For freeing my daughter, Elaine, you shall always have my sword whenever you need it.
King Pelles celebrated Lancelot's brave rescue of Elaine.
But the king also had plans for the noble knight and his lovely daughter.
Lancelot shall soon drink the potion. The prophecy shall come true.
A witch had shown King Pelles a strange vision. Whoever would bear Lancelot's child would give birth to the greatest knight in the world.

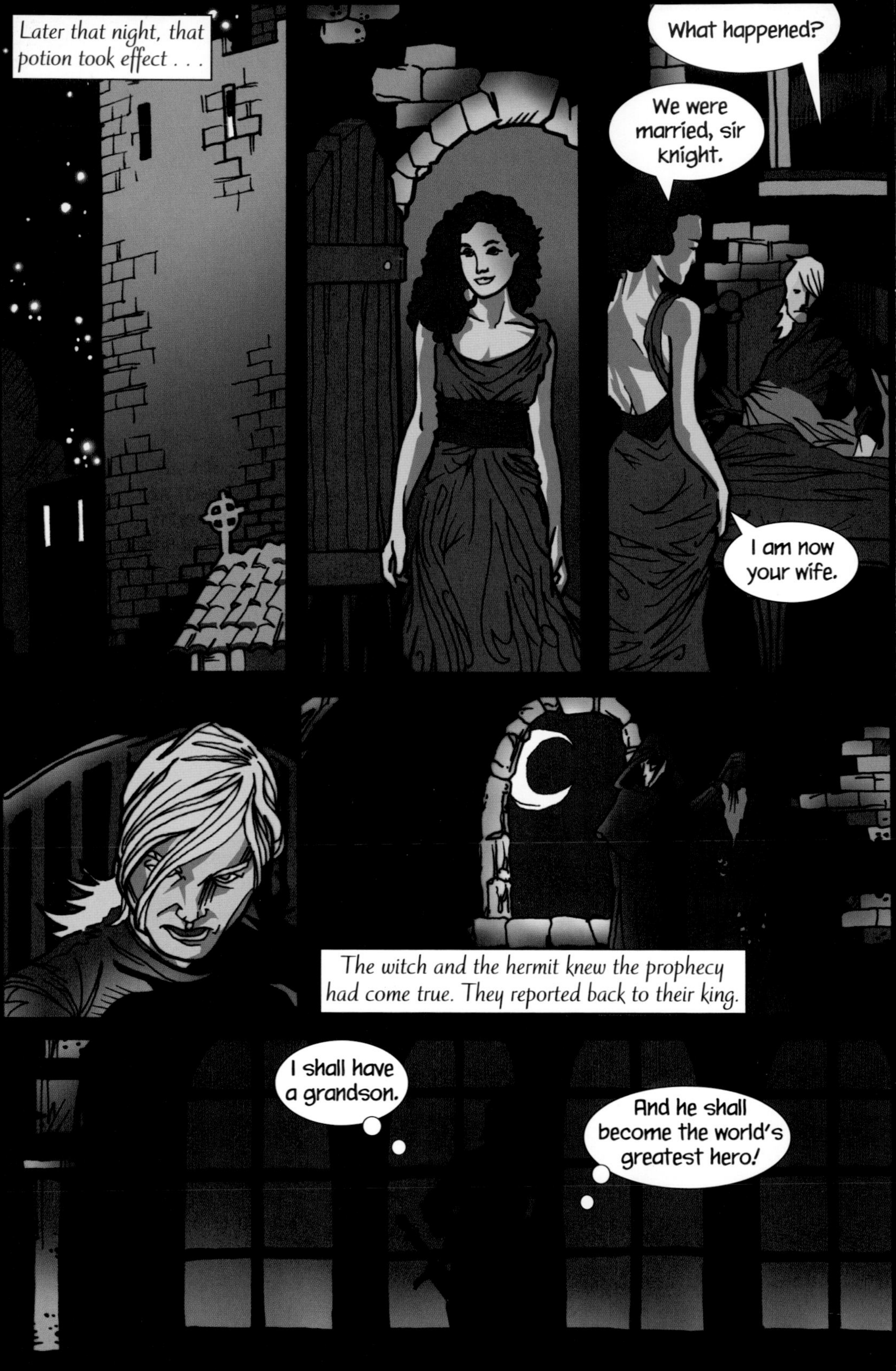
Later that night, that potion took effect . . .
What happened?
We were married, sir knight.
I am now your wife.
The witch and the hermit knew the prophecy had come true. They reported back to their king.
I shall have a grandson.
And he shall become the world's greatest hero!

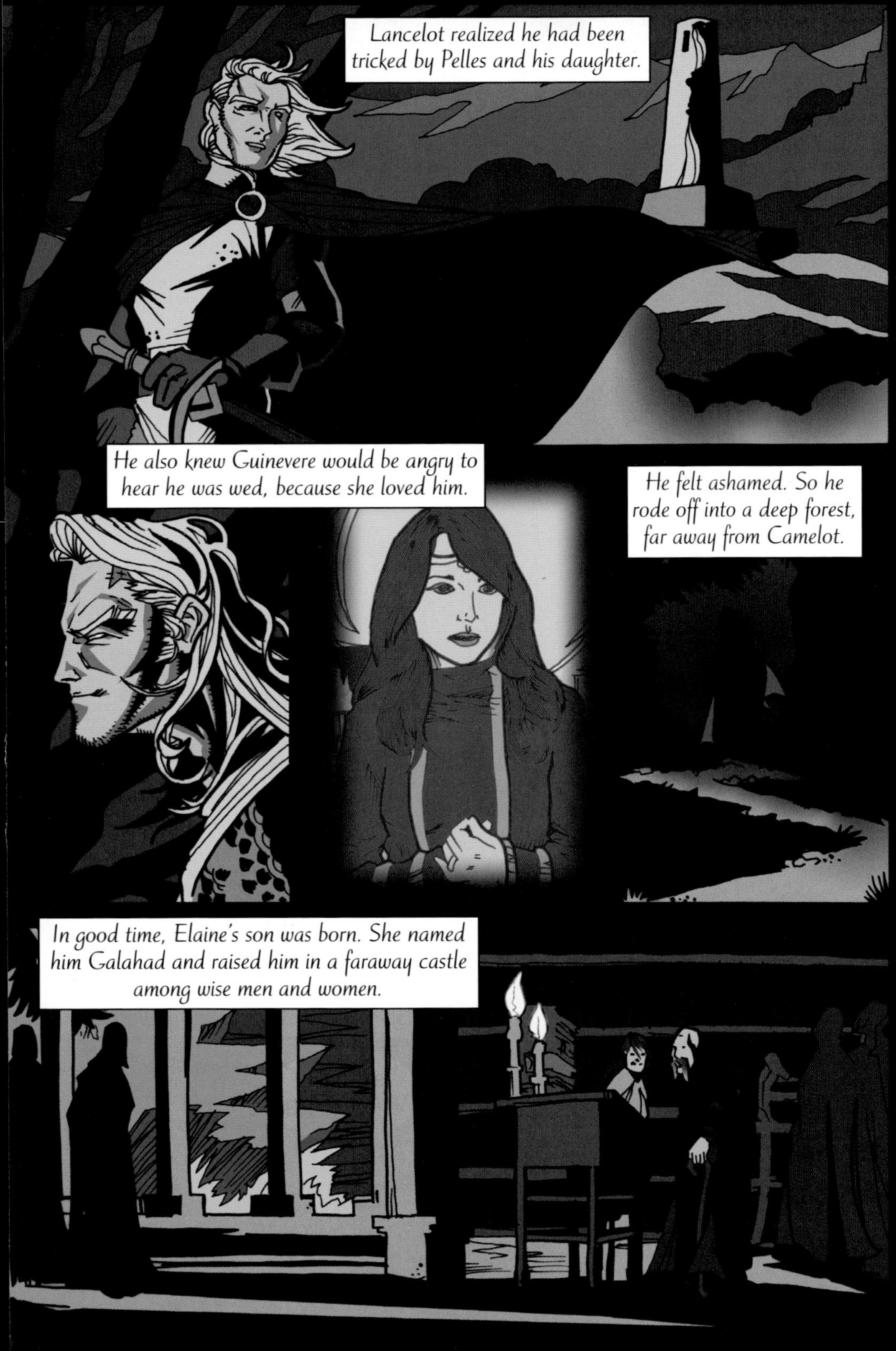
Lancelot realized he had been tricked by Pelles and his daughter.
He also knew Guinevere would be angry to hear he was wed, because she loved him.
He felt ashamed. So he rode off into a deep forest, far away from Camelot.
In good time, Elaine's son was born. She named him Galahad and raised him in a faraway castle among wise men and women.

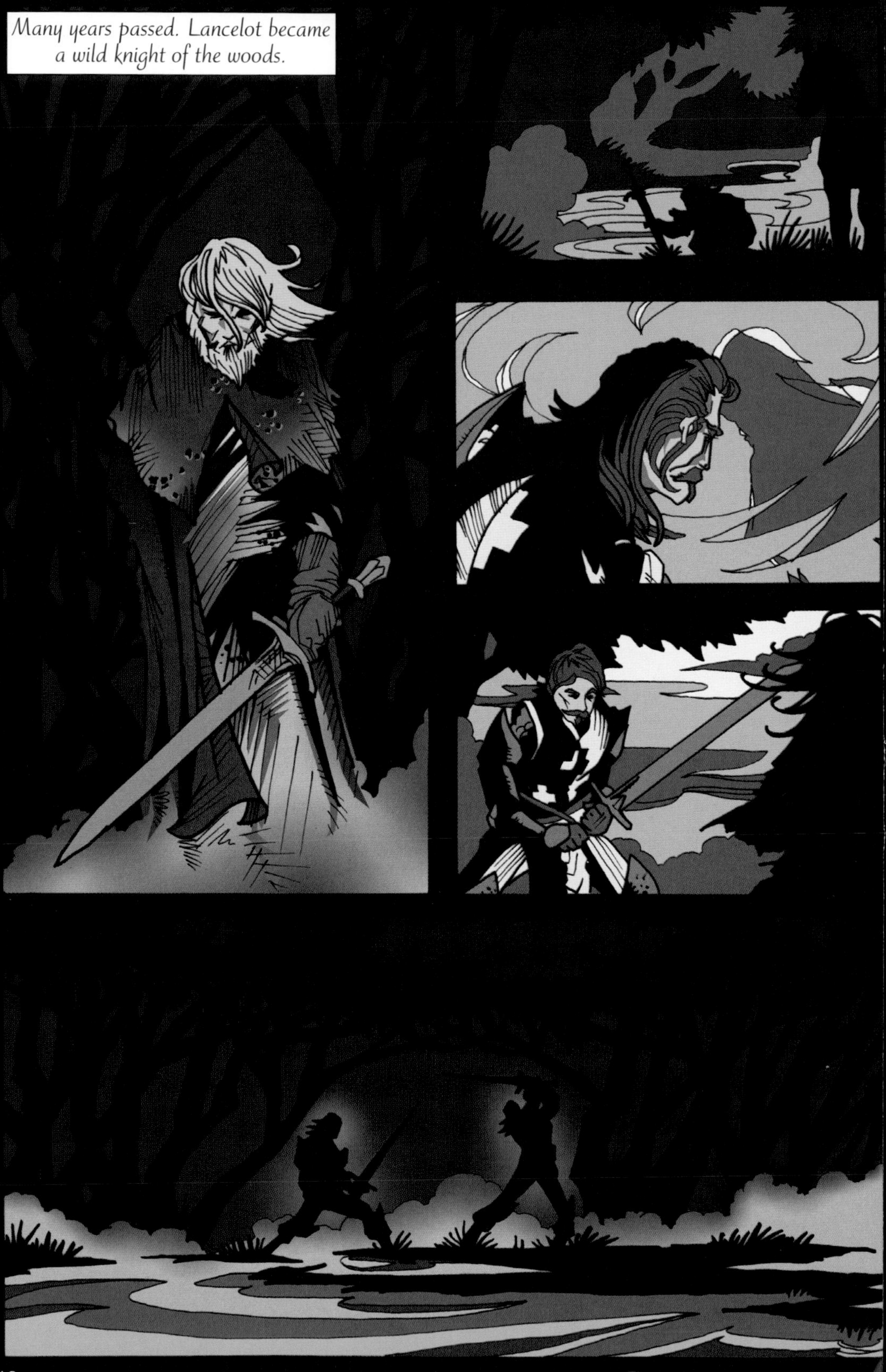
Many years passed. Lancelot became a wild knight of the woods.

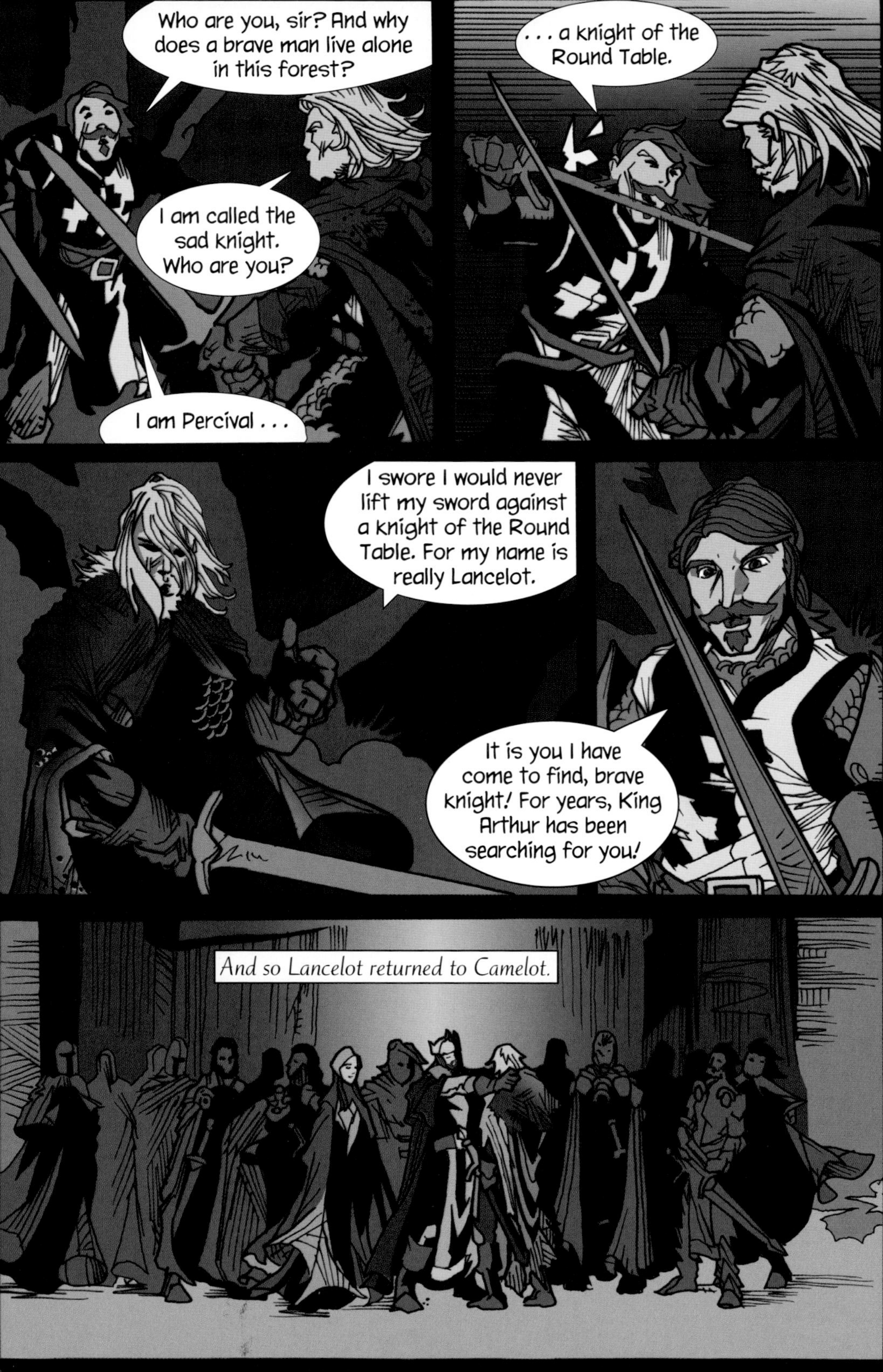
Who are you, sir? And why does a brave man live alone in this forest?
I am called the sad knight. Who are you?
I am Percival . . .
. . . a knight of the Round Table.
I swore I would never lift my sword against a knight of the Round Table. For my name is really Lancelot.
It is you I have come to find, brave knight! For years, King Arthur has been searching for you!
And so Lancelot returned to Camelot.

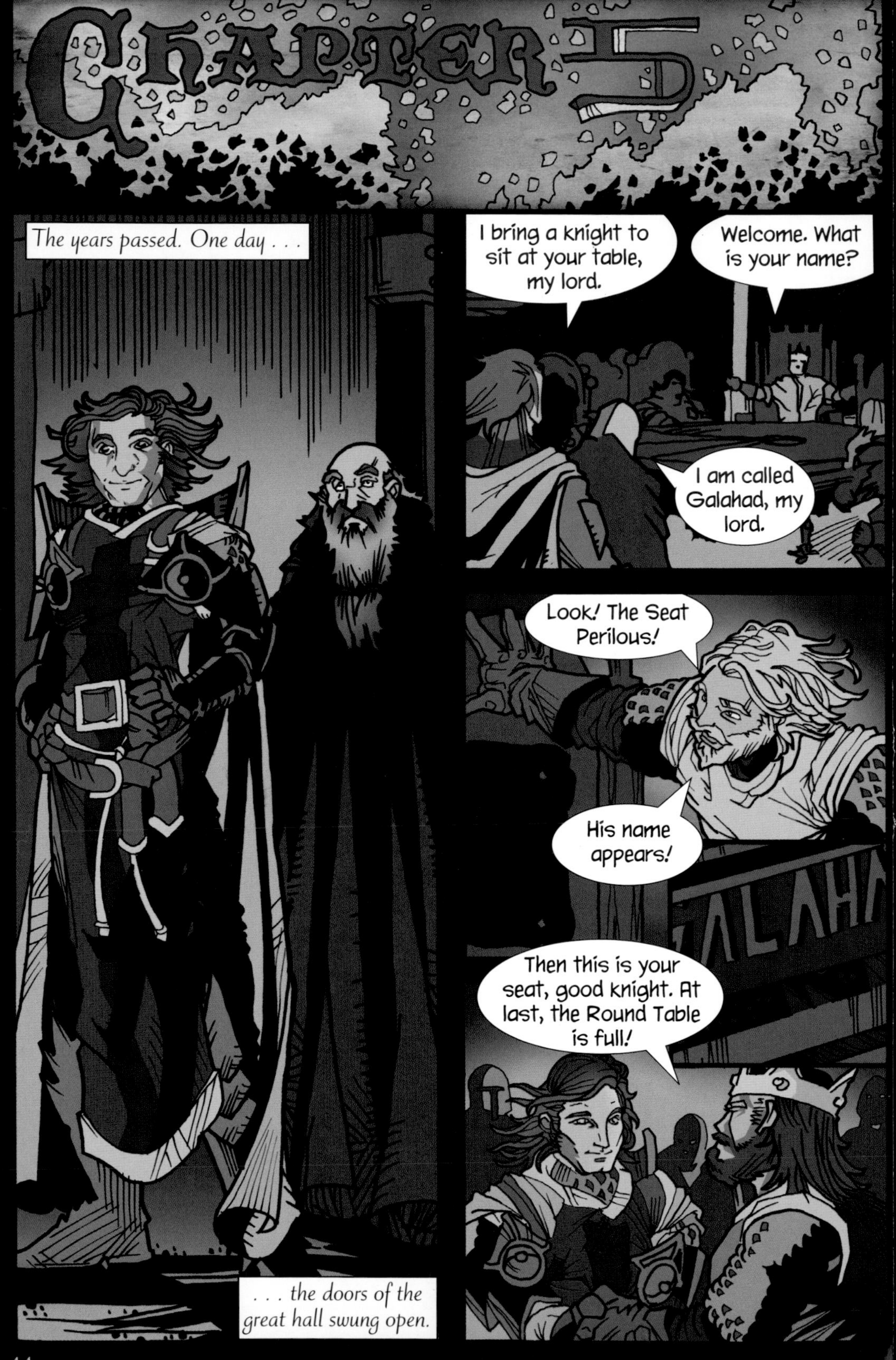
Chapter 5
The years passed. One day . . .
. . . the doors of the great hall swung open.
I bring a knight to sit at your table, my lord.
Welcome. What is your name?
I am called Galahad, my lord.
Look! The Seat Perilous!
His name appears!
Then this is your seat, good knight. At last, the Round Table is full!

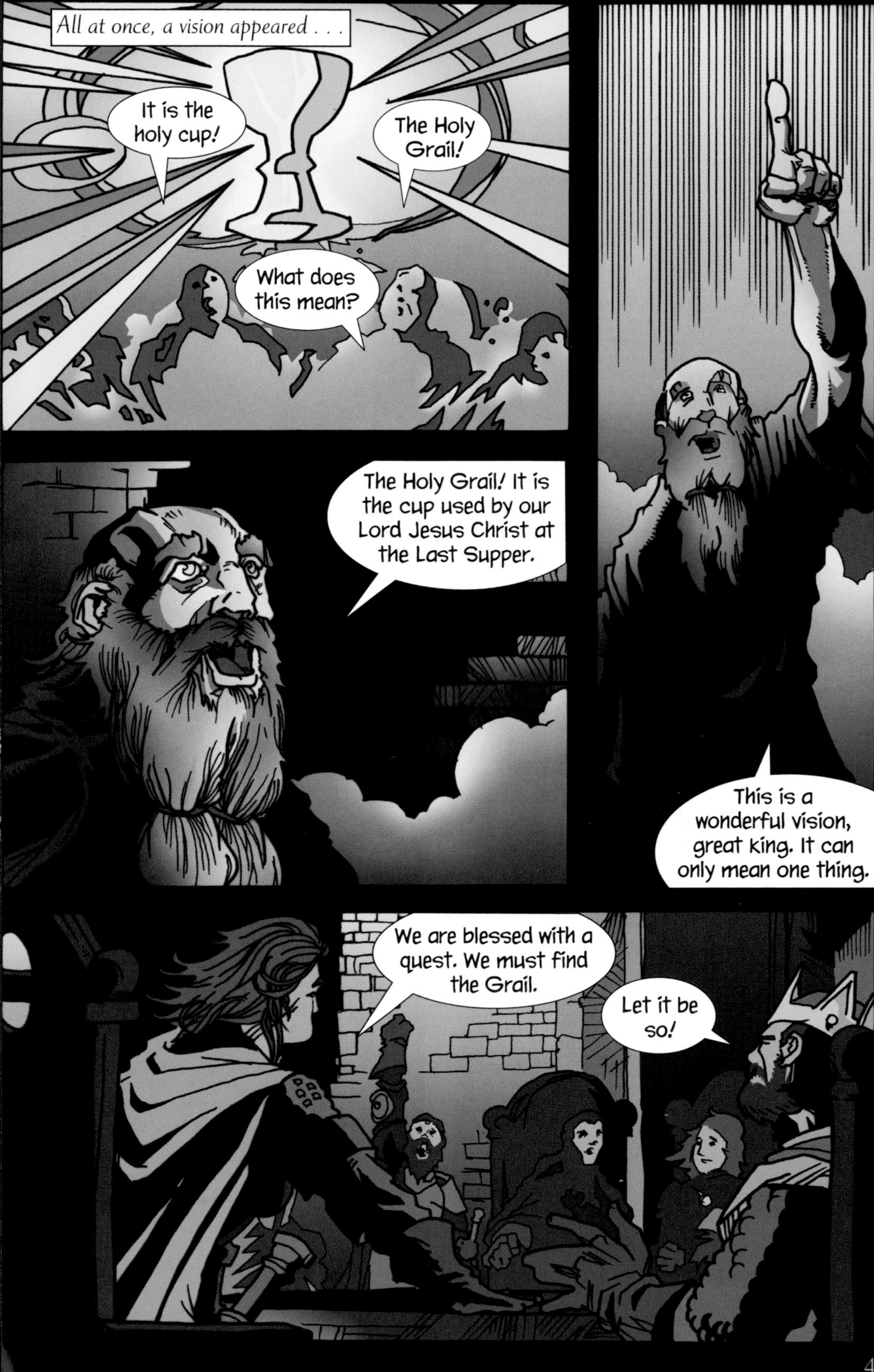
All at once, a vision appeared . . .
It is the holy cup!
The Holy Grail!
What does this mean?
The Holy Grail! It is the cup used by our Lord Jesus Christ at the Last Supper.
This is a wonderful vision, great king. It can only mean one thing.
We are blessed with a quest. We must find the Grail.
Let it be so!

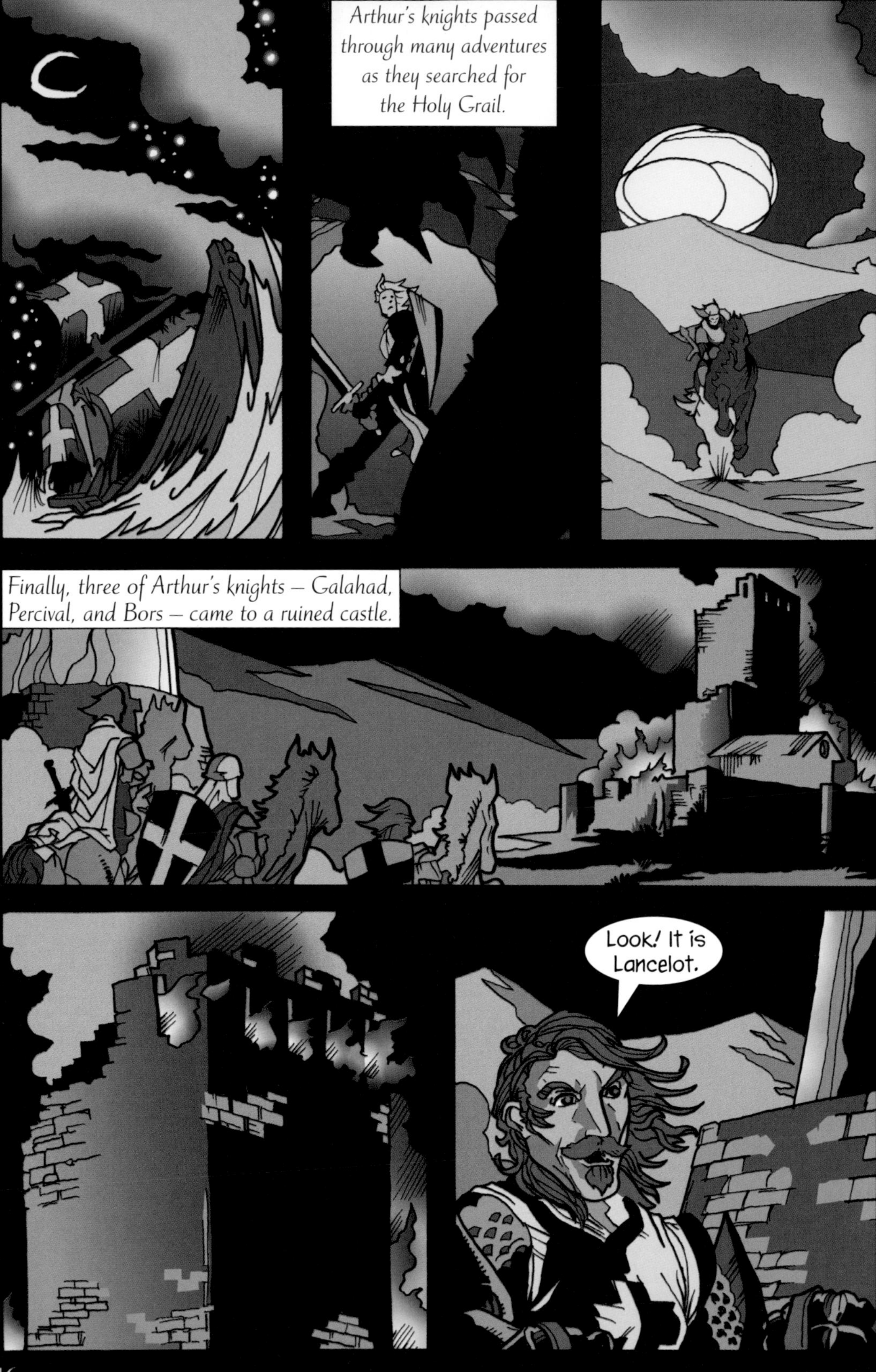
Arthur's knights passed through many adventures as they searched for the Holy Grail.
Finally, three of Arthur's knights – Galahad, Percival, and Bors – came to a ruined castle.
Look! It is Lancelot.

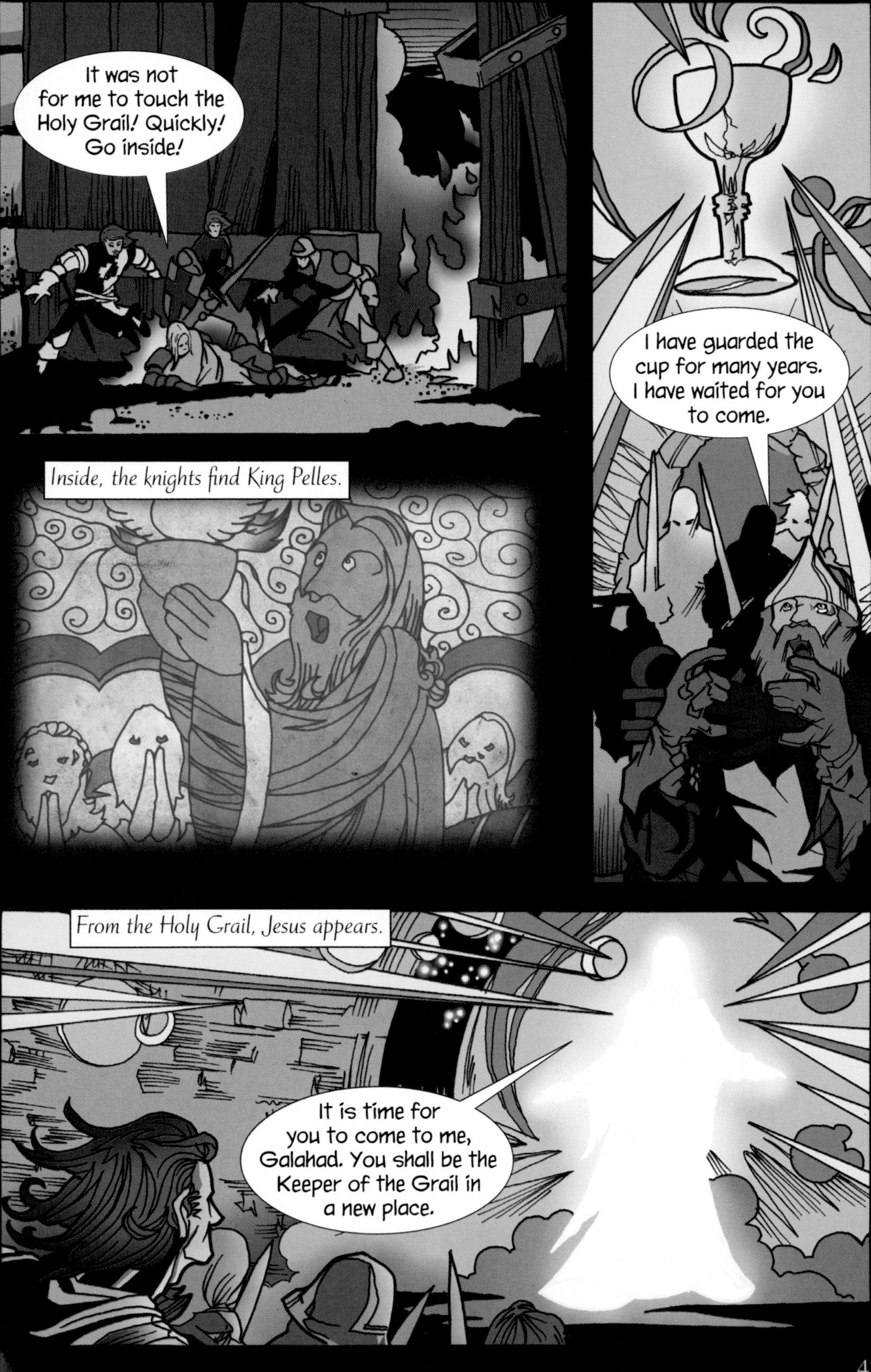
It was not for me to touch the Holy Grail! Quickly! Go inside!
I have guarded the cup for many years. I have waited for you to come.
Inside, the knights find King Pelles.
From the Holy Grail, Jesus appears.
It is time for you to come to me, Galahad. You shall be the Keeper of the Grail in a new place.

Galahad drank from the cup, and then . . .

Galahad and the Grail were never seen again.

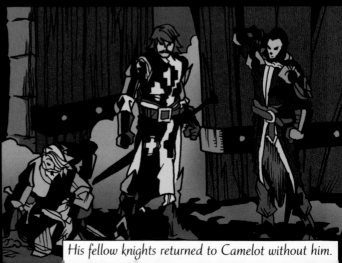

His fellow knights returned to Camelot without him.

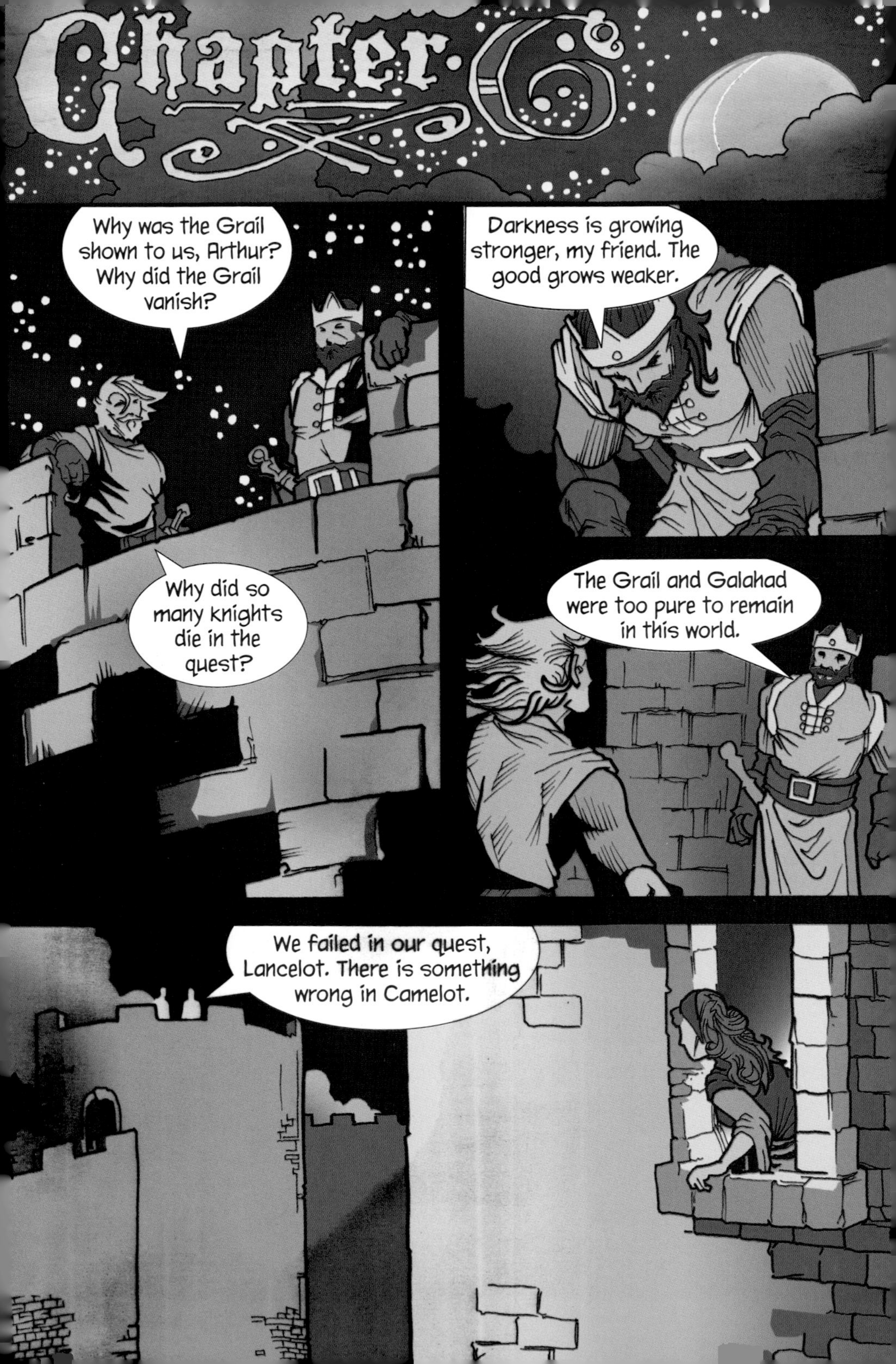
Chapter 6
Why was the Grail shown to us, Arthur? Why did the Grail vanish?
Why did so many knights die in the quest?
Darkness is growing stronger, my friend. The good grows weaker.
The Grail and Galahad were too pure to remain in this world.
We failed in our quest, Lancelot. There is something wrong in Camelot.

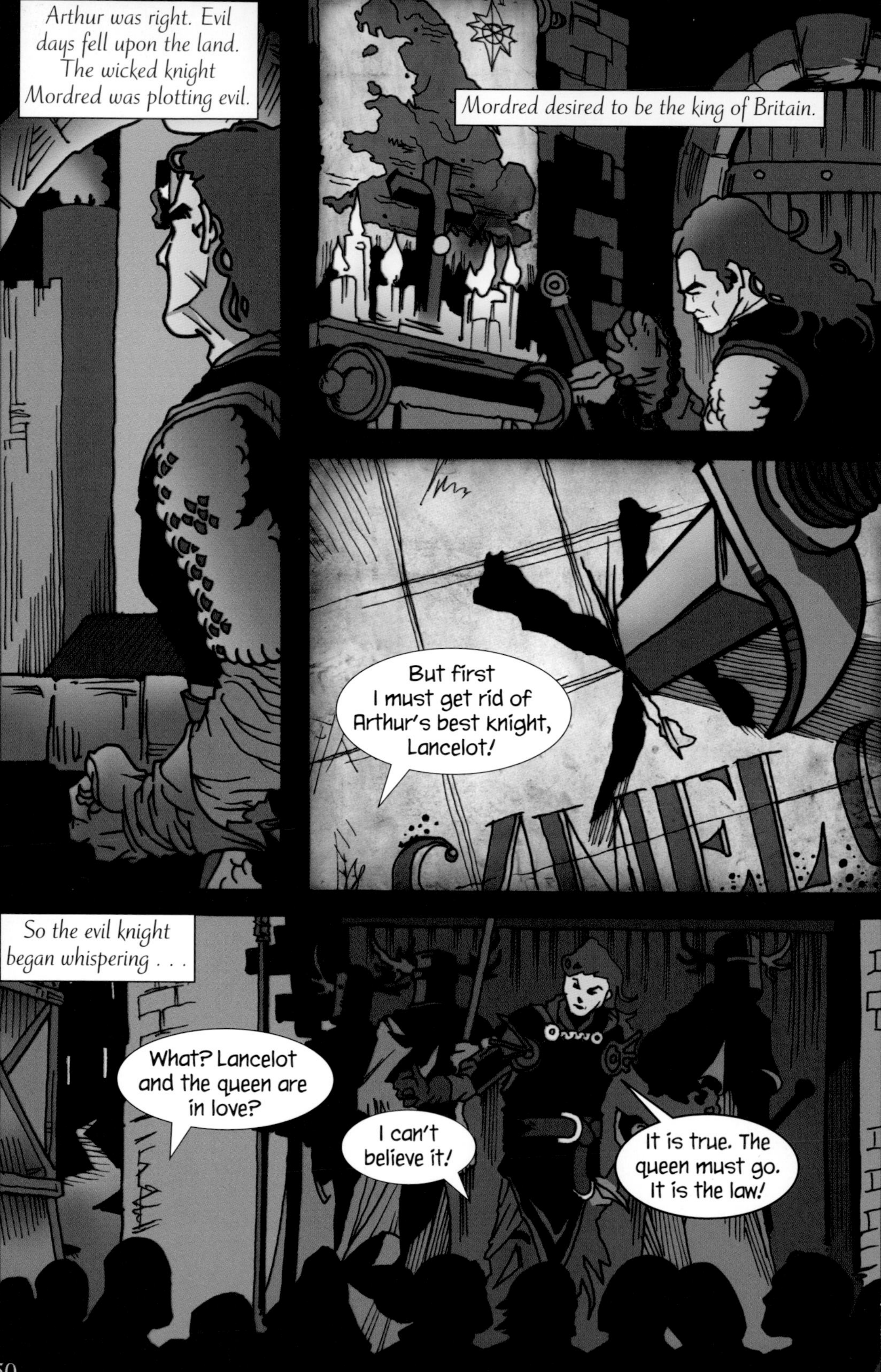
Arthur was right. Evil days fell upon the land. The wicked knight Mordred was plotting evil.
Mordred desired to be the king of Britain.
But first I must get rid of Arthur's best knight, Lancelot!
So the evil knight began whispering . . .
What? Lancelot and the queen are in love?
I can't believe it!
It is true. The queen must go. It is the law!

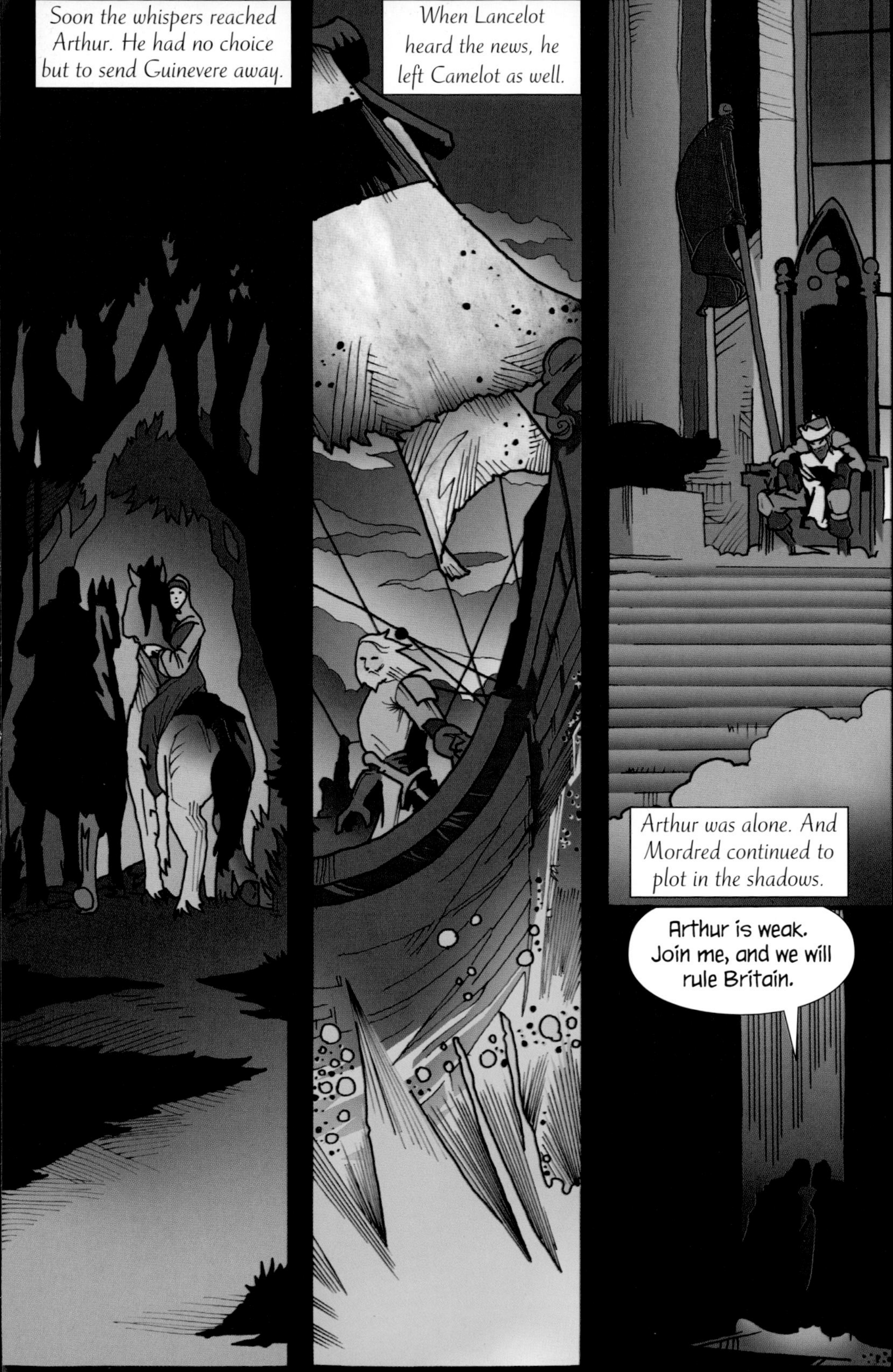
Soon the whispers reached Arthur. He had no choice but to send Guinevere away.
When Lancelot heard the news, he left Camelot as well.
Arthur was alone. And Mordred continued to plot in the shadows.
Arthur is weak. Join me, and we will rule Britain.

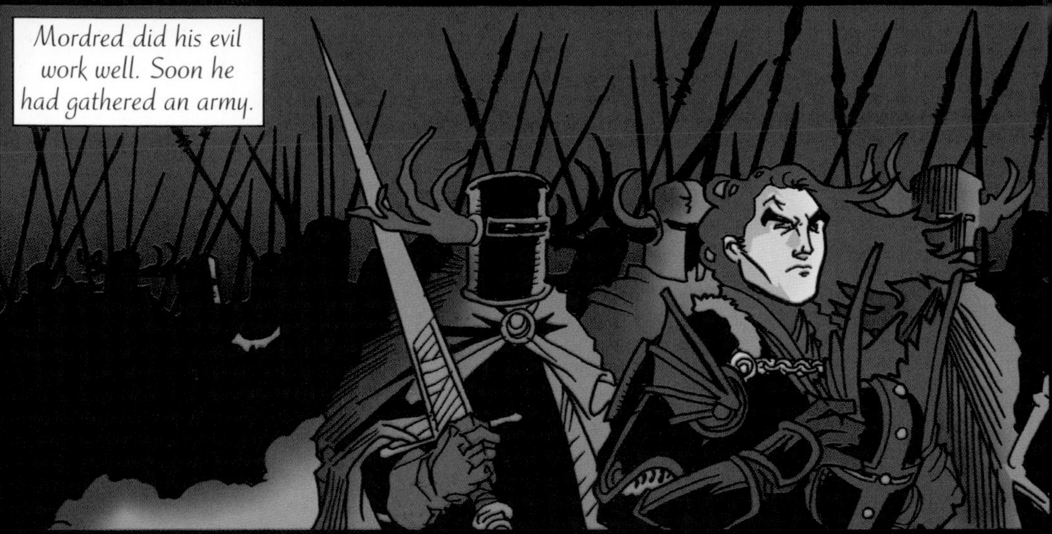
Mordred did his evil work well. Soon he had gathered an army.

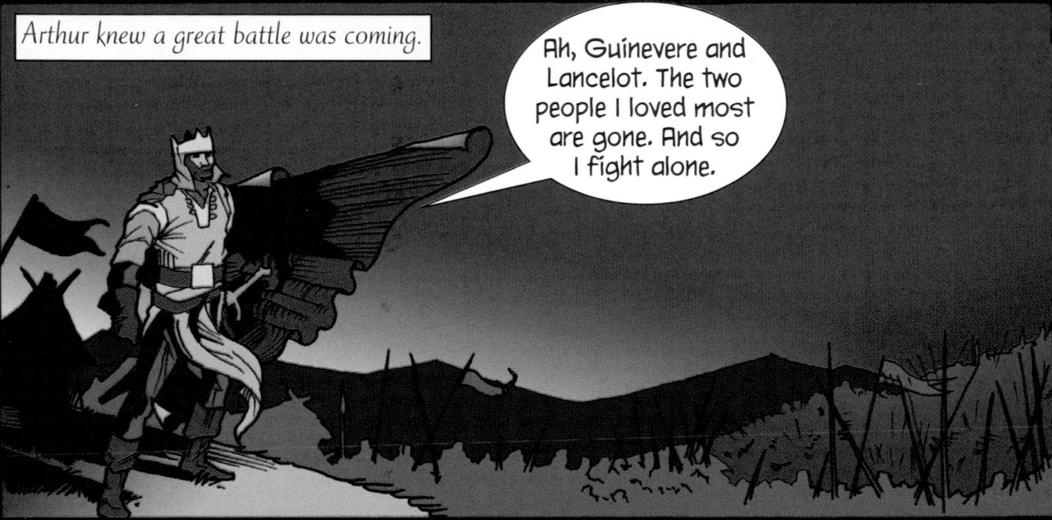
Arthur knew a great battle was coming.
Ah, Guinevere and Lancelot. The two people I loved most are gone. And so I fight alone.

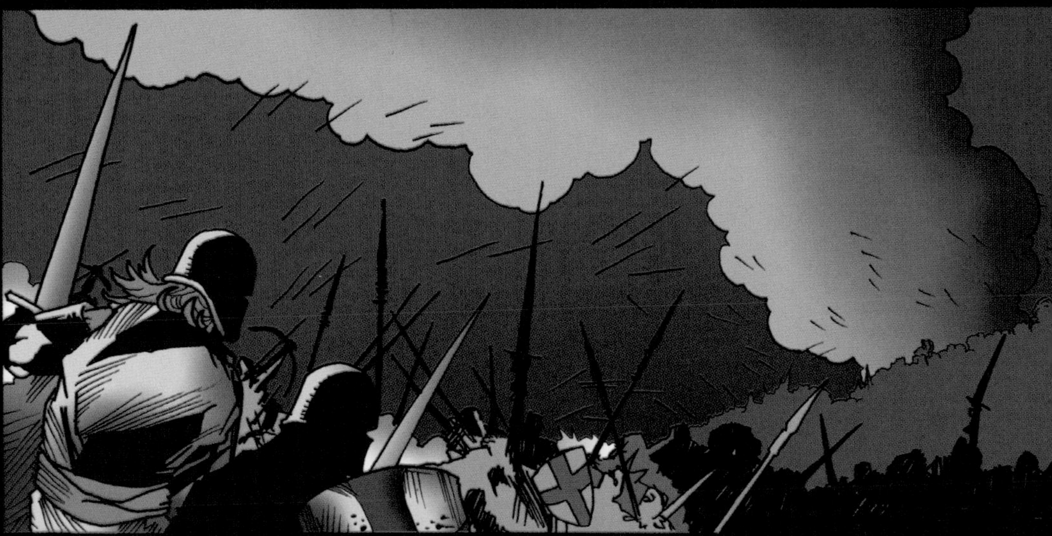

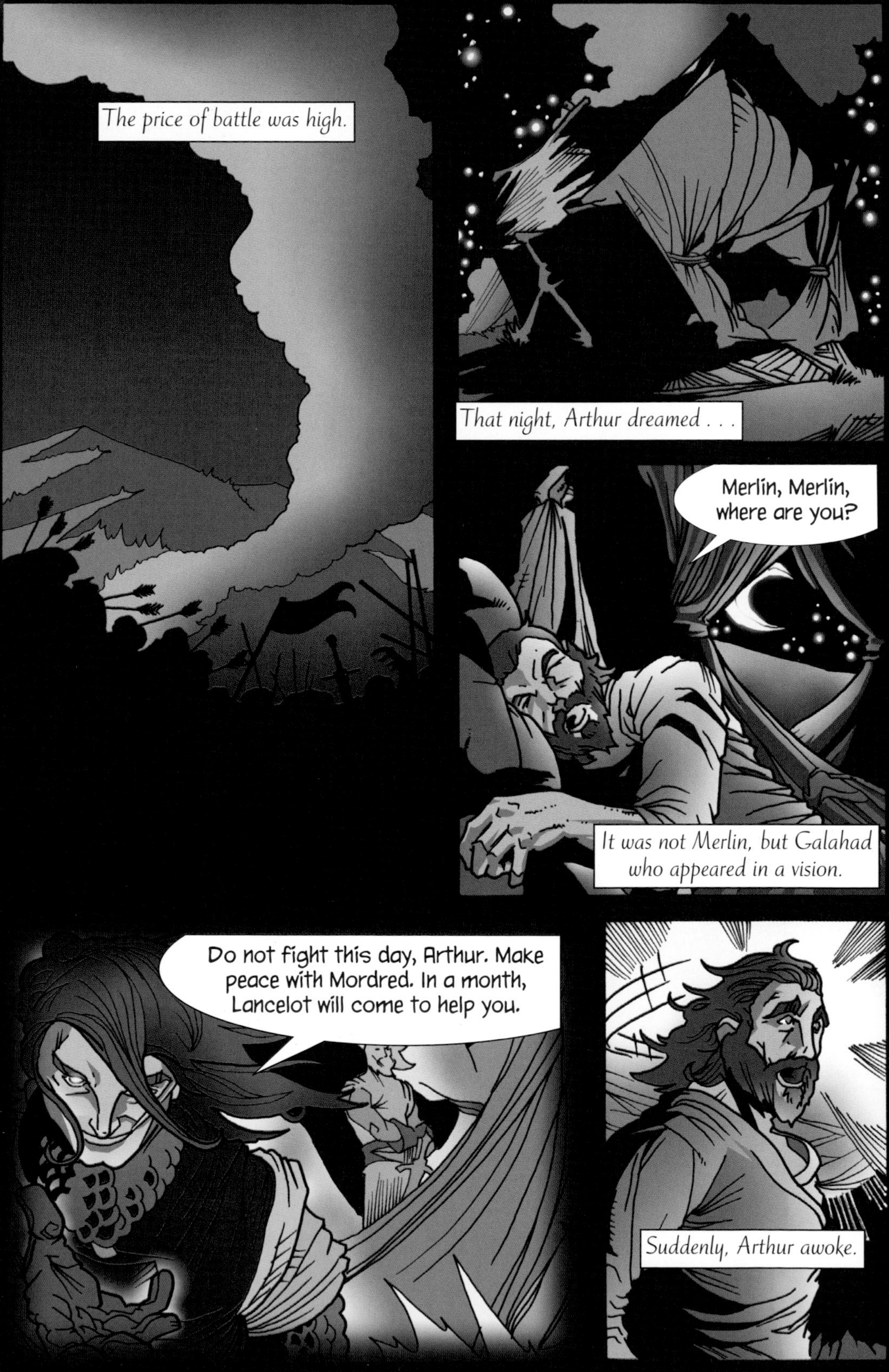
The price of battle was high.
That night, Arthur dreamed . . .
Merlin, Merlin, where are you?
It was not Merlin, but Galahad who appeared in a vision.
Do not fight this day, Arthur. Make peace with Mordred. In a month, Lancelot will come to help you.
Suddenly, Arthur awoke.

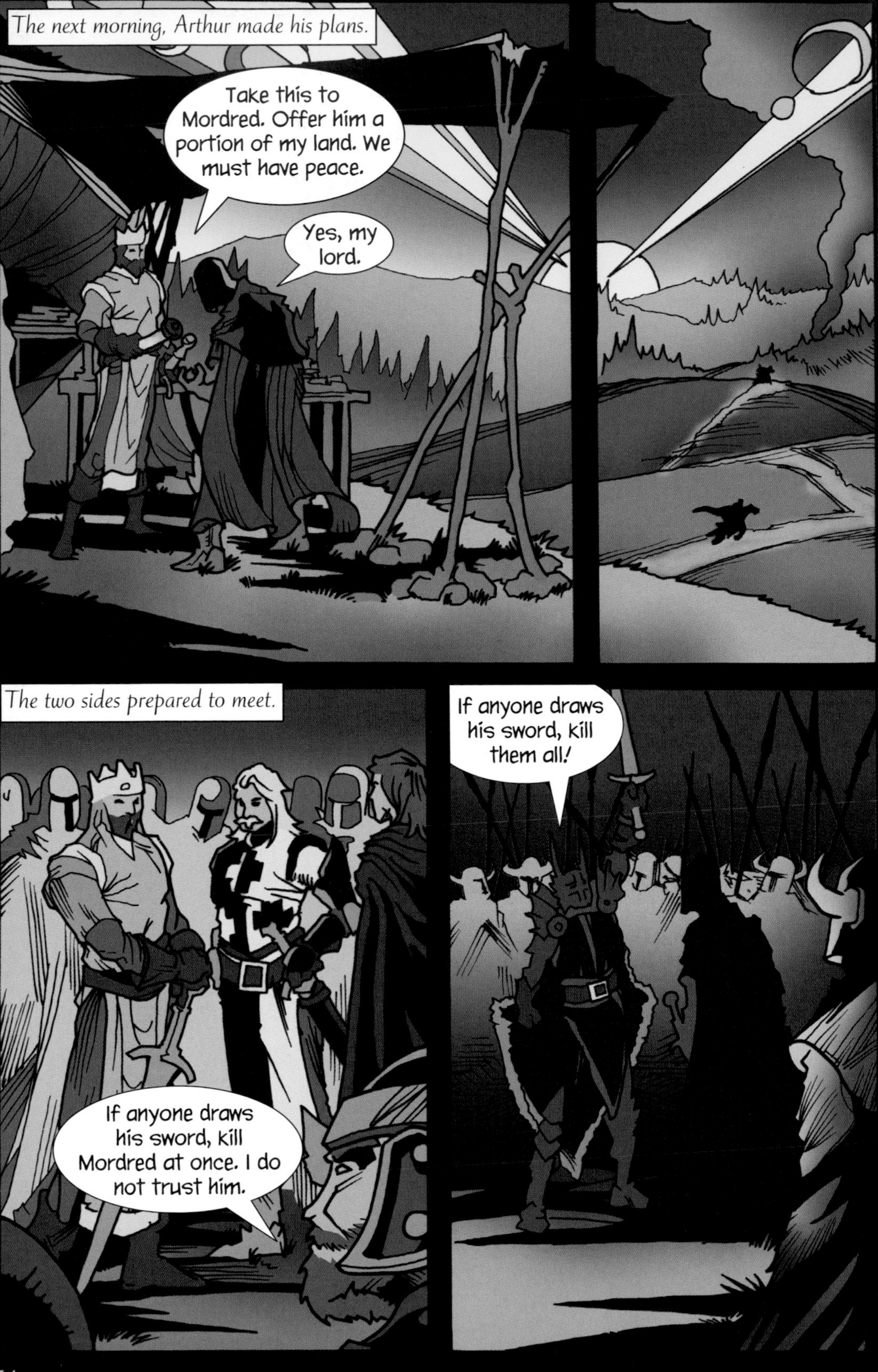
The next morning, Arthur made his plans.
Take this to Mordred. Offer him a portion of my land. We must have peace.
Yes, my lord.
The two sides prepared to meet.
If anyone draws his sword, kill Mordred at once. I do not trust him.
If anyone draws his sword, kill them all!

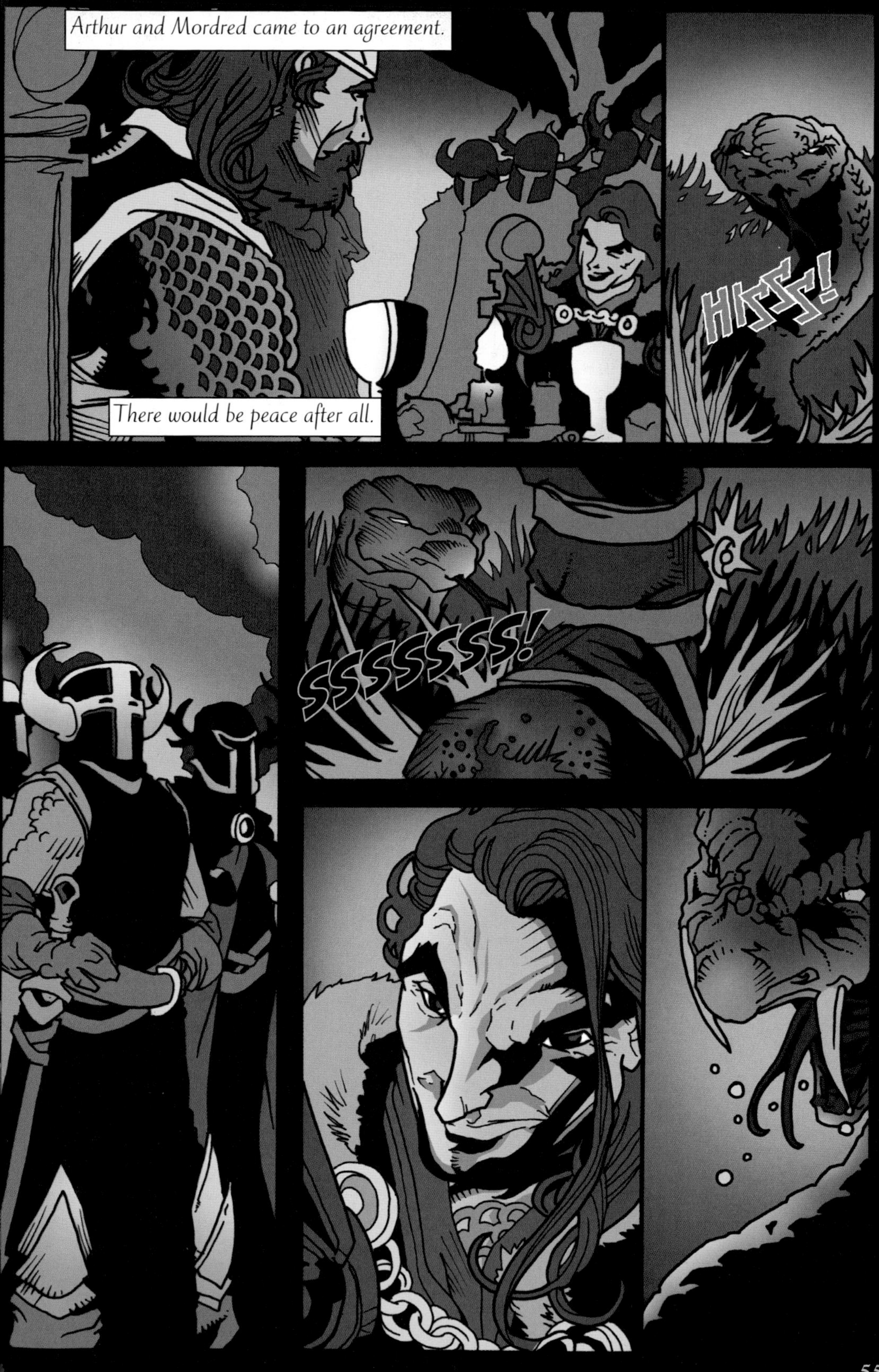
Arthur and Mordred came to an agreement.
There would be peace after all.
HISSS!
SSSSSSS!

But then a snake bit one of Mordred's men.

He drew his sword to kill the snake.

AARGH!

A sword! Charge!

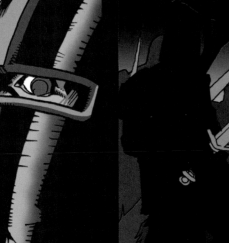

Both armies rushed into battle.

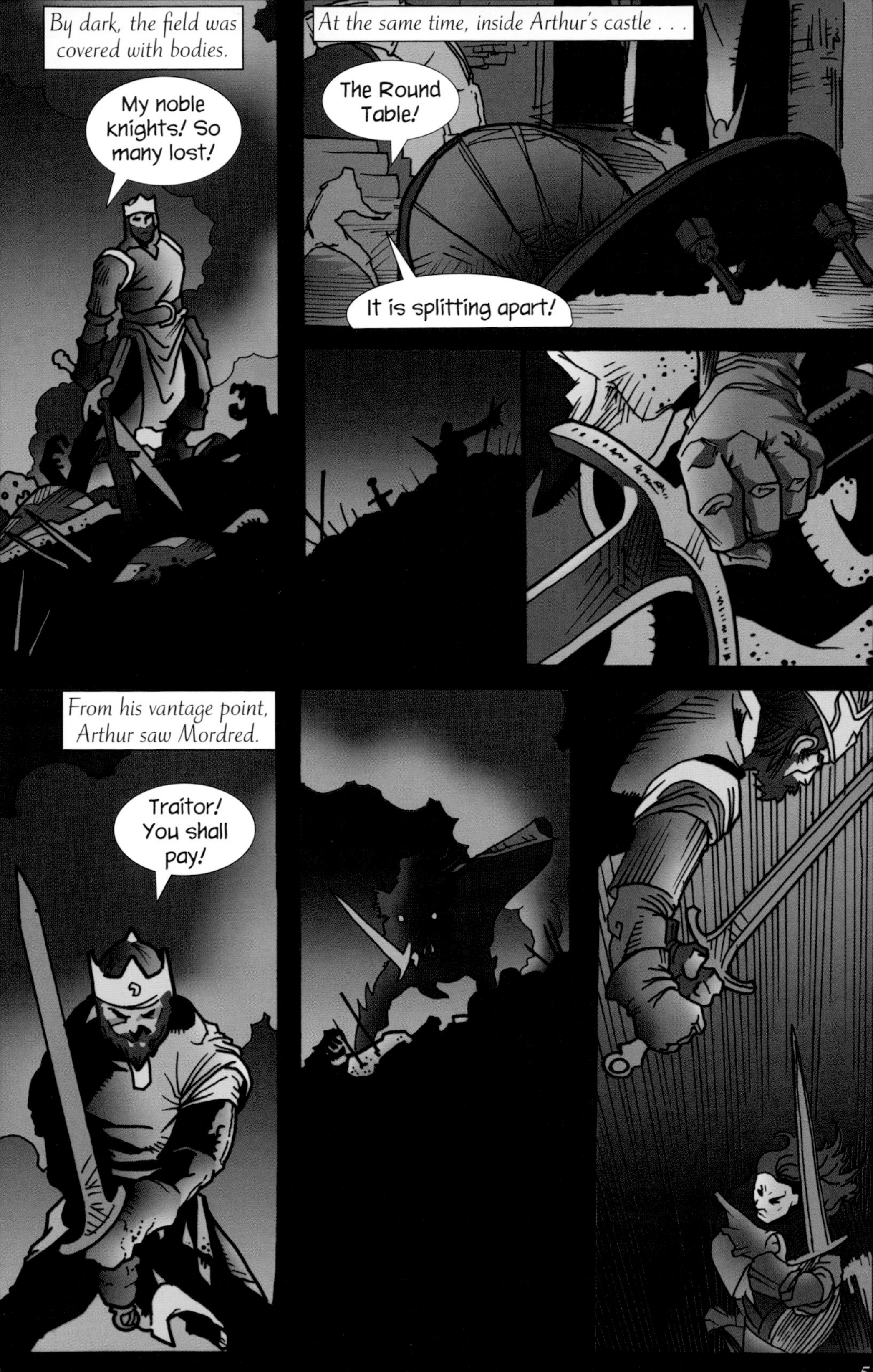

By dark, the field was covered with bodies.
My noble knights! So many lost!
At the same time, inside Arthur's castle . . .
The Round Table!
It is splitting apart!
From his vantage point, Arthur saw Mordred.
Traitor! You shall pay!

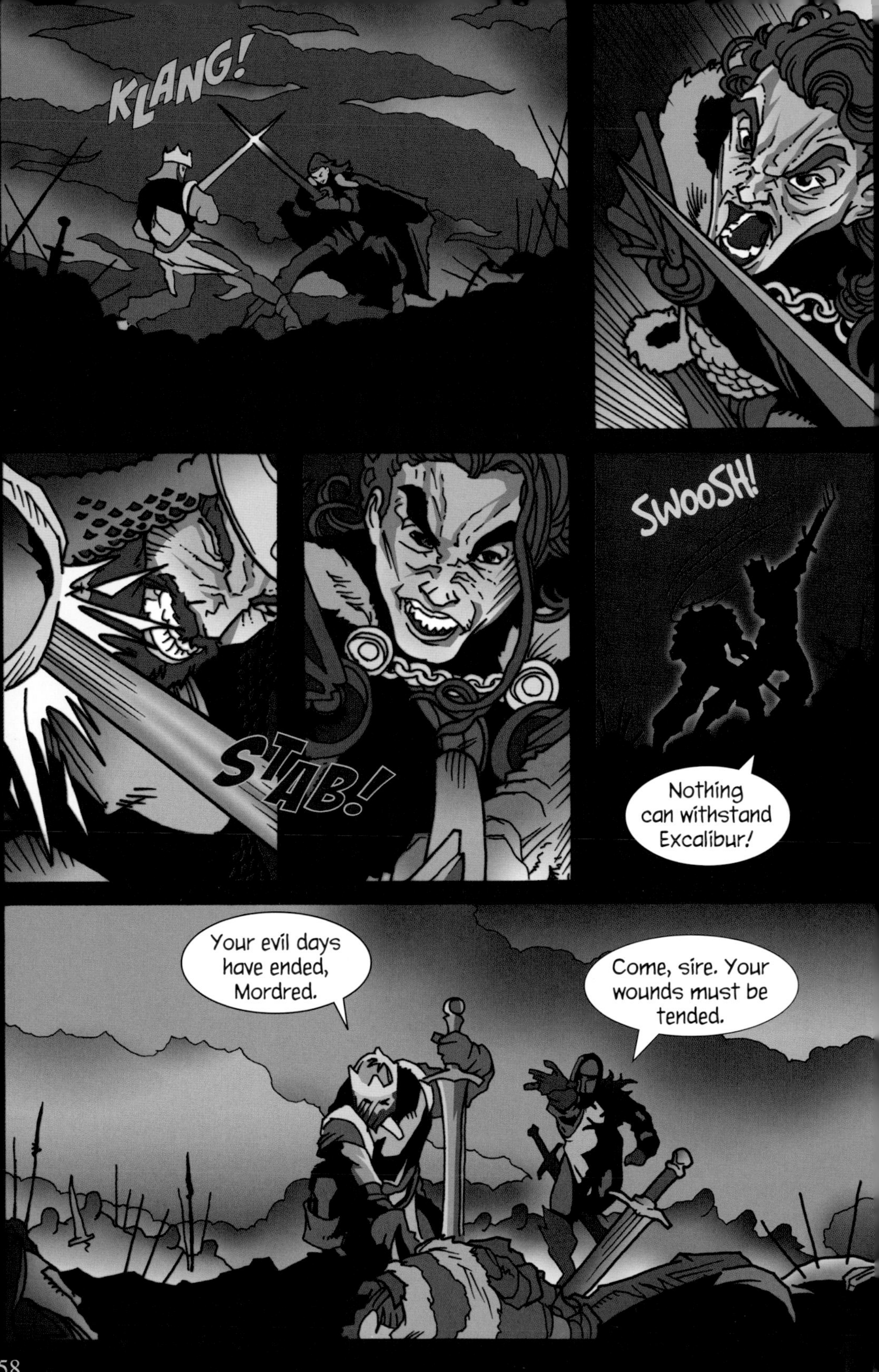
KLANG!
STAB!
SWOOSH!
Nothing can withstand Excalibur!
Your evil days have ended, Mordred.
Come, sire. Your wounds must be tended.

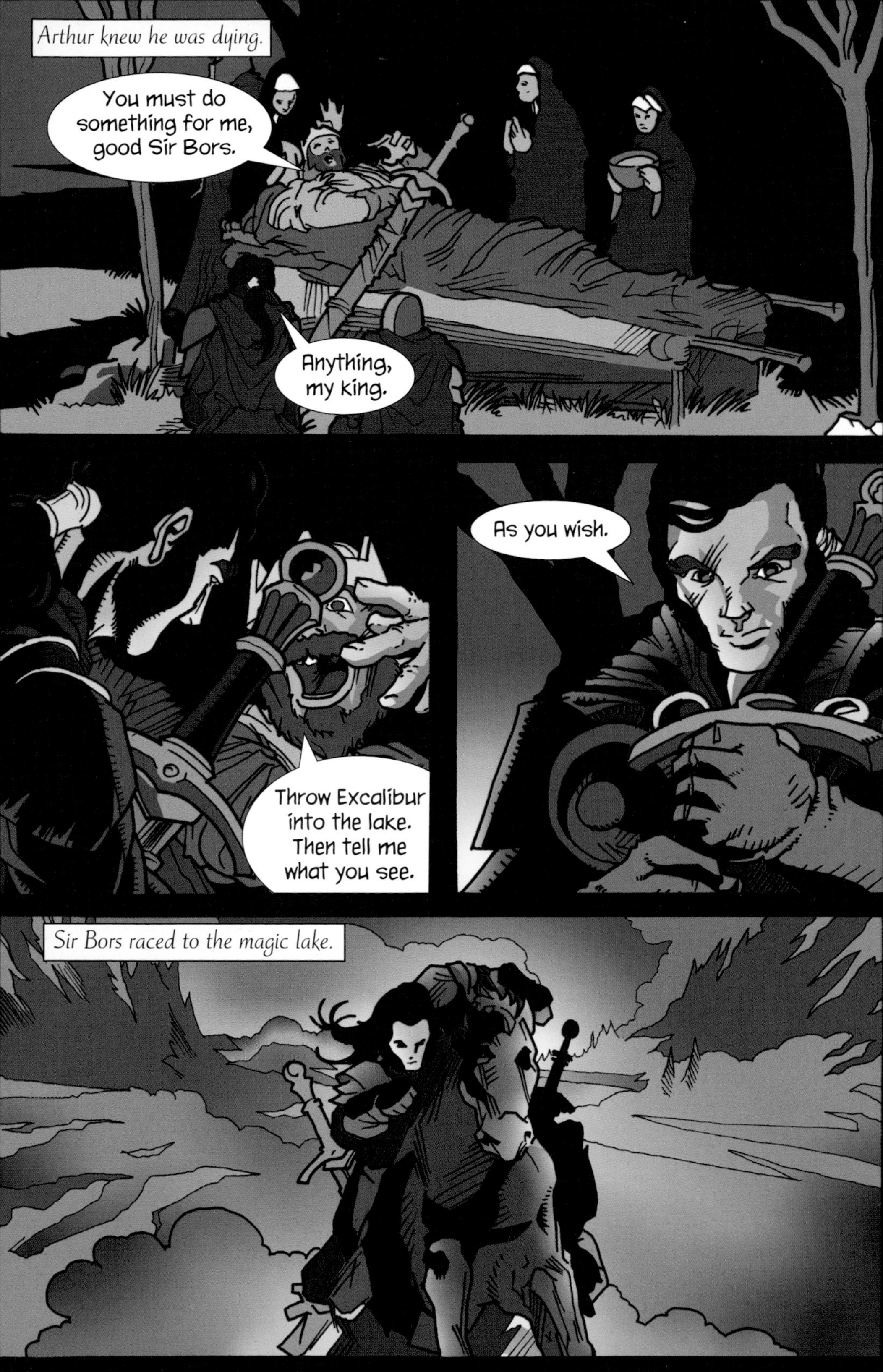

Arthur knew he was dying.
You must do something for me, good Sir Bors.
Anything, my king.
Throw Excalibur into the lake. Then tell me what you see.
As you wish.
Sir Bors raced to the magic lake.

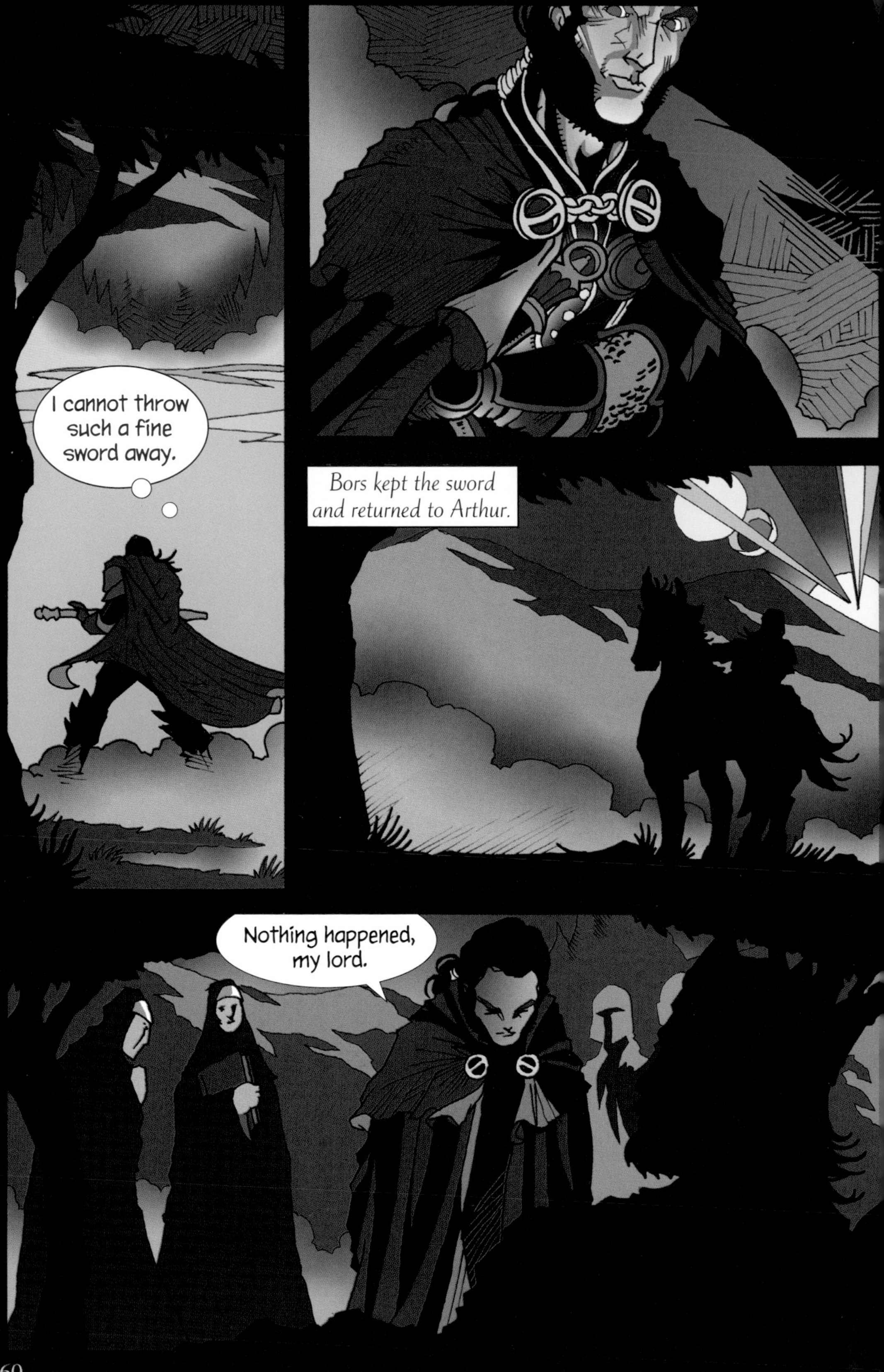
I cannot throw such a fine sword away.
Bors kept the sword and returned to Arthur.
Nothing happened, my lord.

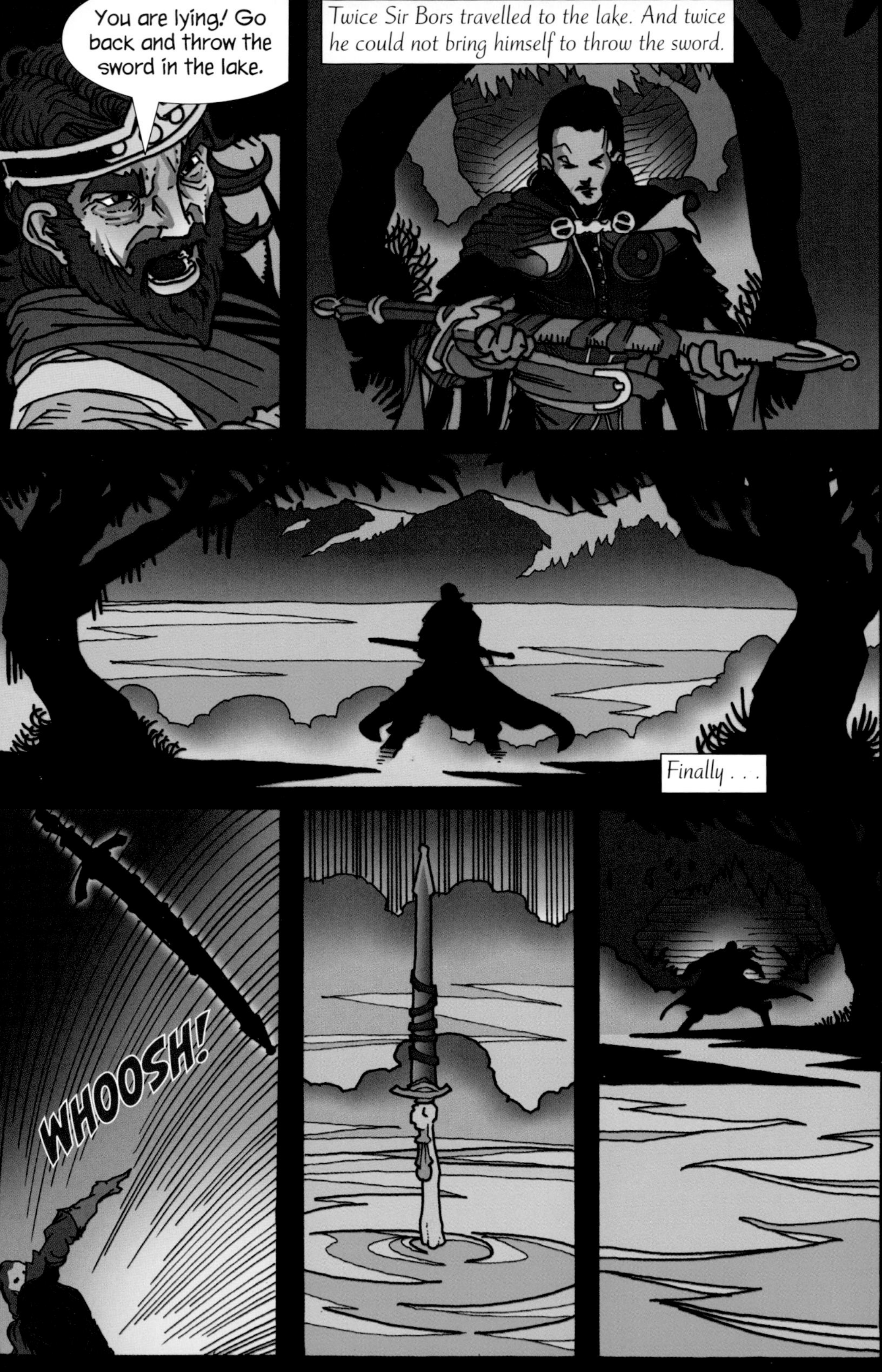
You are lying! Go back and throw the sword in the lake.
Twice Sir Bors travelled to the lake. And twice he could not bring himself to throw the sword.
Finally . . .
WHOOSH!

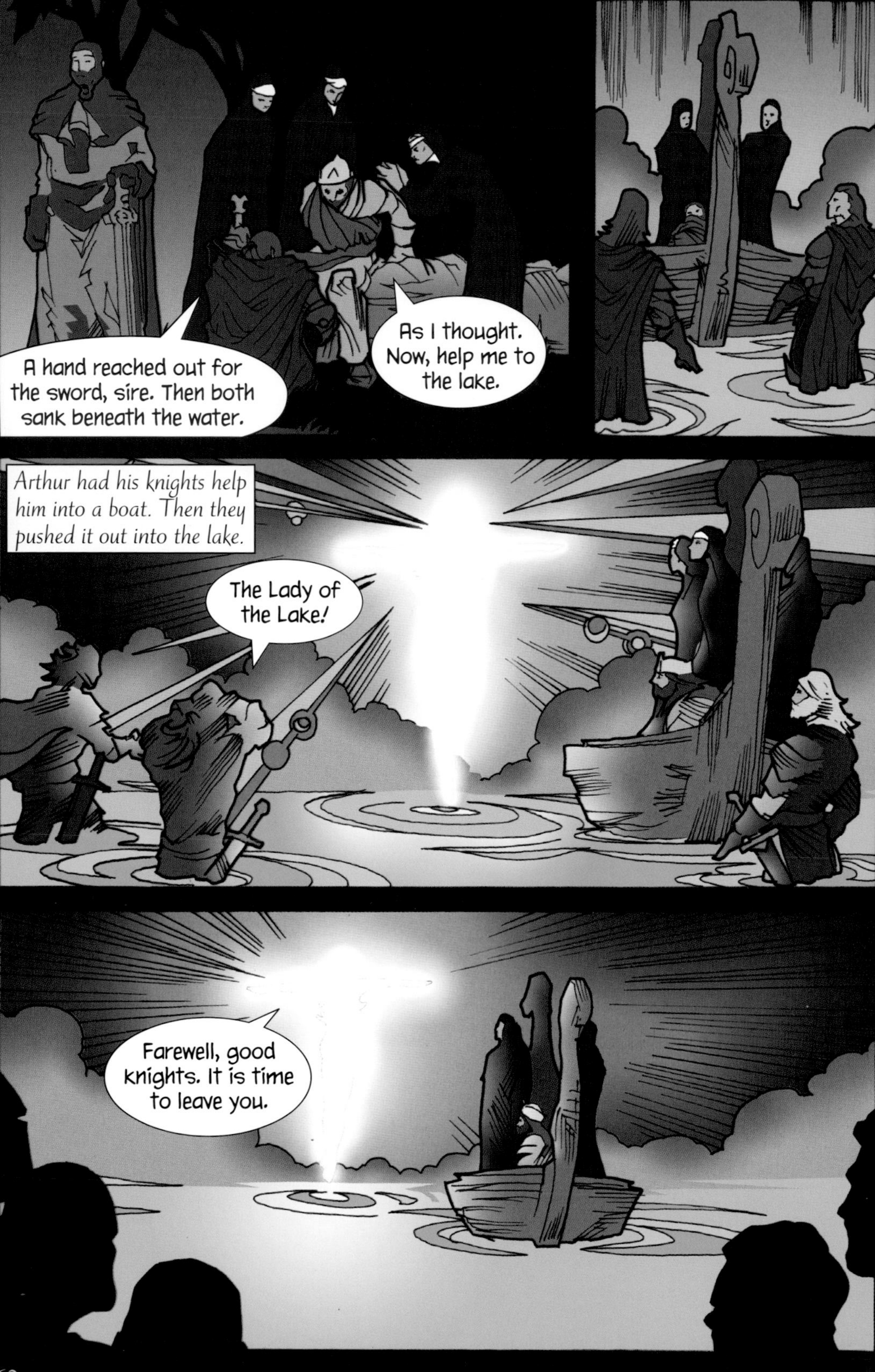
A hand reached out for the sword, sire. Then both sank beneath the water.
As I thought. Now, help me to the lake.
Arthur had his knights help him into a boat. Then they pushed it out into the lake.
The Lady of the Lake!
Farewell, good knights. It is time to leave you.

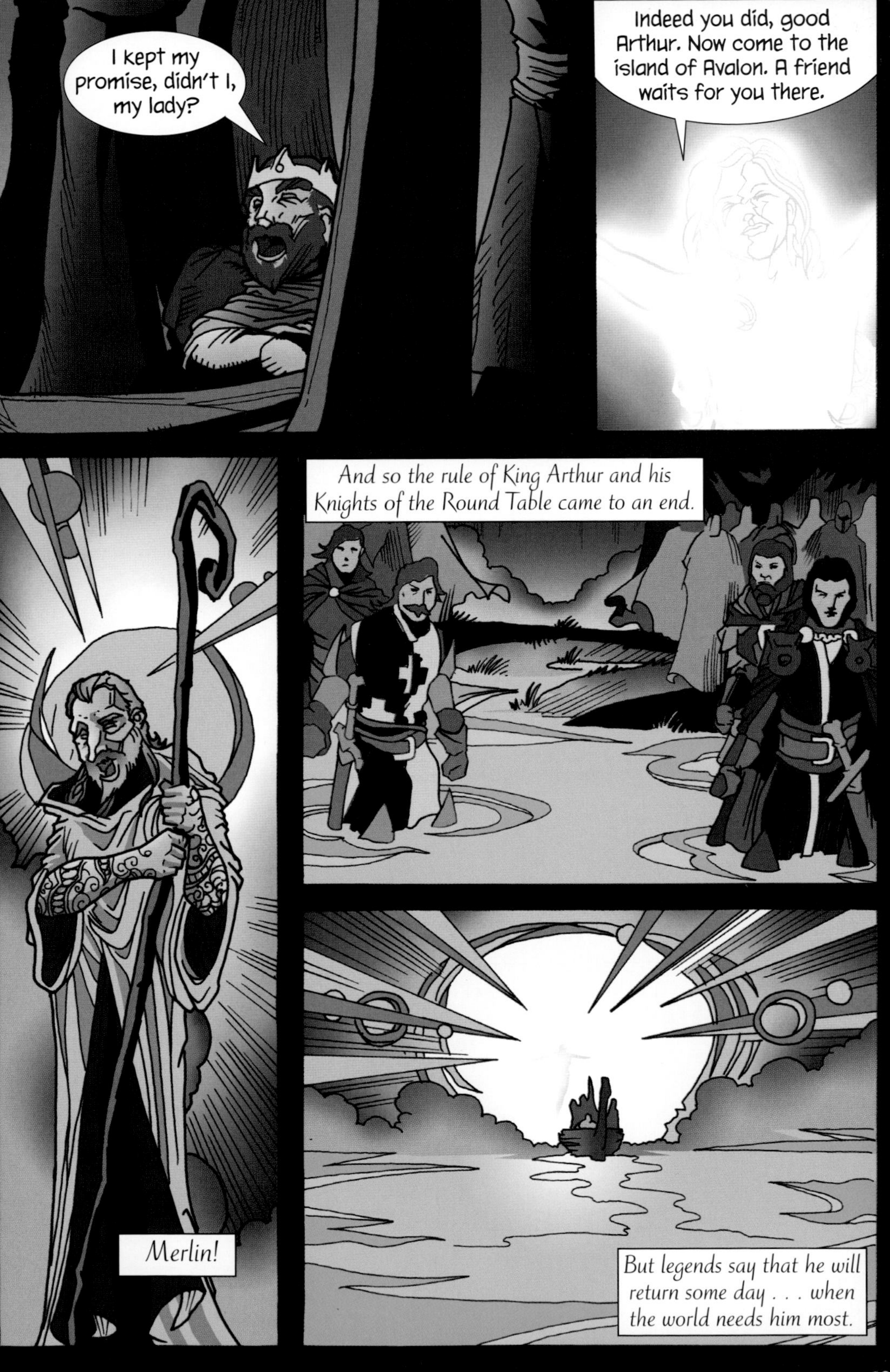

I kept my promise, didn't I, my lady?
Indeed you did, good Arthur. Now come to the island of Avalon. A friend waits for you there.
Merlin!
And so the rule of King Arthur and his Knights of the Round Table came to an end.
But legends say that he will return some day . . . when the world needs him most.

ABOUT SIR THOMAS MALORY

The story of King Arthur is an ancient legend that storytellers passed down for many generations. The story was first told sometime before the 11th century. Finally, in the 15th century, Sir Thomas Malory wrote down his version of these stories. He titled the collection *The Book of King Arthur and His Noble Knights of the Round Table.*

People know little about Malory's interest in the stories of King Arthur. He likely heard different versions of these stories when he was growing up. Perhaps his life experience as a knight helped him better understand the good and evil forces in the King Arthur stories.

ABOUT THE AUTHOR

M. C. Hall has written more than 80 fiction and non-fiction books for children, including science books, biographies, and fairy tales. She likes to read, walk on the beach, garden, and ski. She lives in Boston, USA.

ABOUT THE ILLUSTRATOR

C. E. Richards grew up reading comic books, C. S. Lewis, J. R. R. Tolkien, and watching *Star Wars*. He is a graduate of Savannah College of Art and lives in Atlanta, USA, where he is working on book and magazine illustrations, comic books, poster design, playbill illustration, and album artwork for CDs.

GLOSSARY

archbishop (arch-BISH-up) – the ruler of bishops in some Christian religions

duke (DYOOK) – in Britain, a person ranked lower than a prince

fortress (FOR-truhss) – a group of buildings protected by walls and forts

hermit (HUR-mit) – a person who lives alone and away from others

joust (JOWST) – a battle with lances or spears fought between knights on horseback

moat (MOHT) – a deep, wide ditch filled with water that surrounds a castle or fortress and keeps people away

perilous (PARE-uhl-uhss) – dangerous

potion (PO-shuhn) – a drink with special powers

prophesy (PROF-uh-see) – a prediction

rebel (REB-uhl) – a person who doesn't follow rules

scabbard (SKAB-urd) – a case that people wear to hold a sword

wizard (WIZ-urd) – a person with magical powers

BACKGROUND ON THE KNIGHTS OF THE ROUND TABLE

The stories of King Arthur and the Knights of the Round Table take place in Britain during the Middle Ages, a time period that lasted from the 5th to the 15th century CE. This was a period of unrest in Britain and Europe as people fought many wars for control of the land. Britain wasn't a united country at the time.

Kings and lords throughout what is now England, Wales, and Scotland ruled over small regions scattered across the countryside.

Many people wonder if the legends of King Arthur are real and if the places in the story really existed. Some historians believe that the castle of Camelot and the island of Avalon are based on real places in England. For example, some people believe that Arthur is buried beneath the town of Glastonbury. Visitors still travel to England to retrace the steps of King Arthur and his knights.

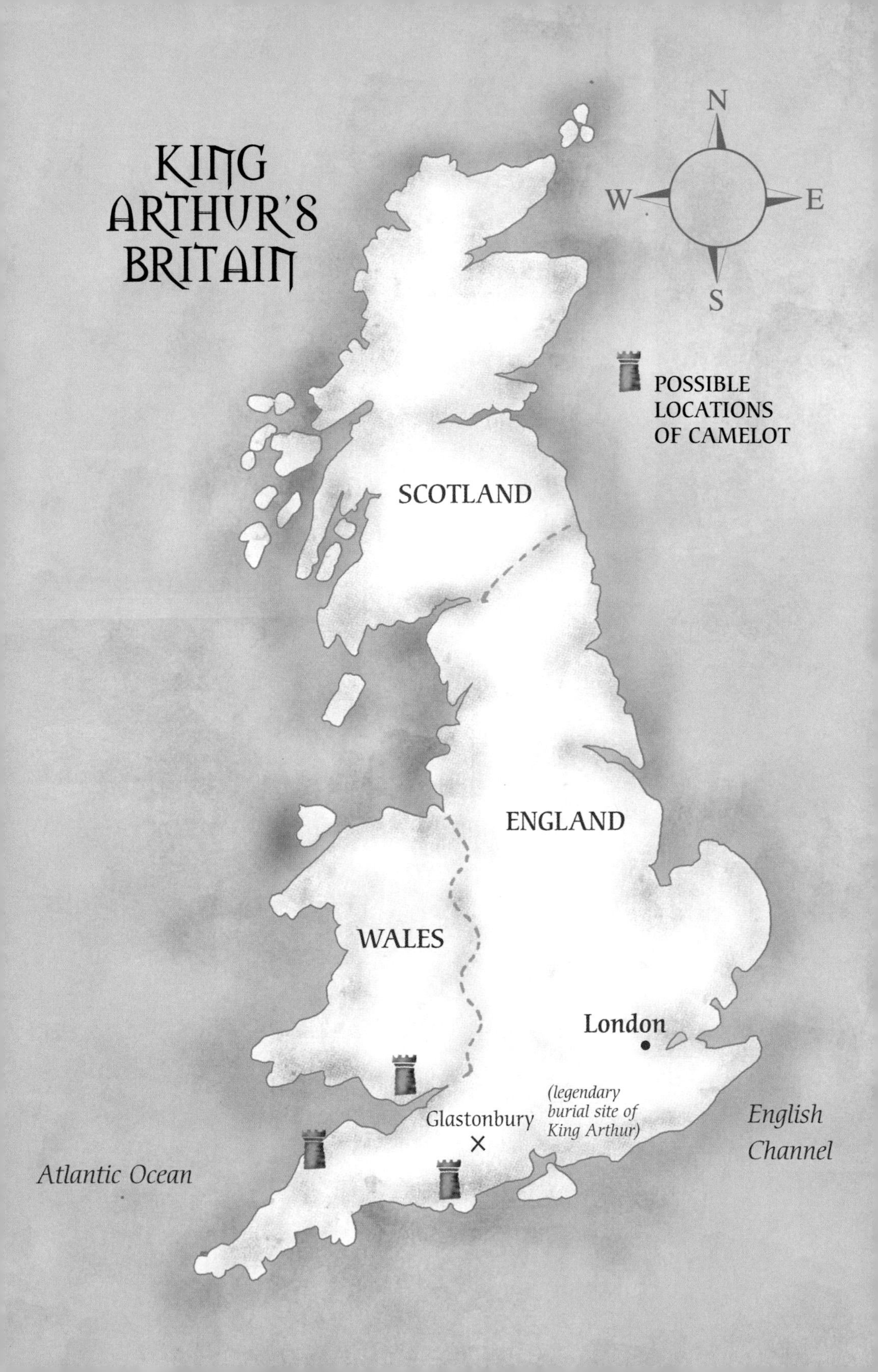
KING ARTHUR'S BRITAIN
N
W
E
S
POSSIBLE LOCATIONS OF CAMELOT
SCOTLAND
ENGLAND
WALES
London
Glastonbury
(legendary burial site of King Arthur)
English Channel
Atlantic Ocean

DISCUSSION QUESTIONS

1. Why did the Round Table break into two pieces?

2. At the end of the story, we find out that King Arthur and the Knights of the Round Table will return some day. Name some times when you could use the help of Arthur and the knights.

3. Would you like to go back to the times of King Arthur? Why or why not?

4. When Arthur was a boy, how did people know that he was really the king?

WRITING PROMPTS

1. Imagine that you were given the sword Excalibur. Explain what you would do with its magical powers. (Remember, the sword can only be used for good.)

2. Describe your favourite character in the story. Is it Arthur or Guinevere? Lancelot or Merlin? What does your favourite character look like? Why do you like this character the best?

3. The Knights of the Round Table go on a quest to find the Holy Grail. Their journey took a long time. Write about a quest, or journey, that you went on. What did you find at the end of it?

OTHER BOOKS

Black
BEAUTY

Black Beauty

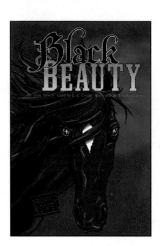

Black Beauty, a handsome colt living in Victorian England, had a happy childhood growing up in the peaceful countryside. In his later years, he encounters terrible illness and a frightening stable fire. Things go from bad to worse when Black Beauty's new owners begin renting him out for profit. Black Beauty endures a life of mistreatment and disrespect in a world that shows little regard for the wellbeing of animals.

THE
HUNCHBACK
OF NOTRE DAME

The Hunchback of Notre Dame

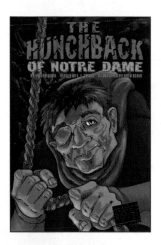

Hidden away in the bell tower of the Cathedral of Notre Dame, Quasimodo is treated like a beast. Although he is gentle and kind, he has the reputation of a frightening monster because of his physical deformities. He develops affection for Esmeralda, a gypsy girl who shows him kindness in return. When the girl is sentenced to an unfair death by hanging, Quasimodo is determined to save her. But those closest to Quasimodo have other plans for the gypsy.

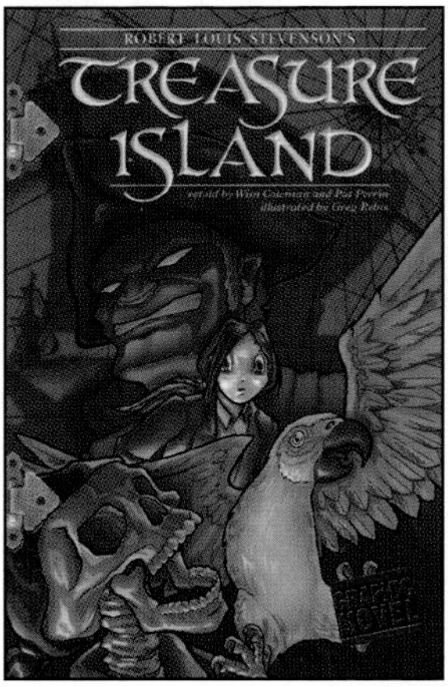
ROBERT LOUIS STEVENSON'S
TREASURE ISLAND

Treasure Island

Jim Hawkins had no idea what he was getting into when the pirate Billy Bones showed up at the doorstep of his mother's inn. When Billy dies suddenly, Jim is left to unlock his old sea chest, which reveals money, a journal, and a treasure map. Joined by a band of honourable men, Jim sets sail on a dangerous voyage to locate the loot on a faraway island. The violent sea is only one of the dangers they face. They soon encounter a band of bloodthirsty pirates determined to make the treasure their own!

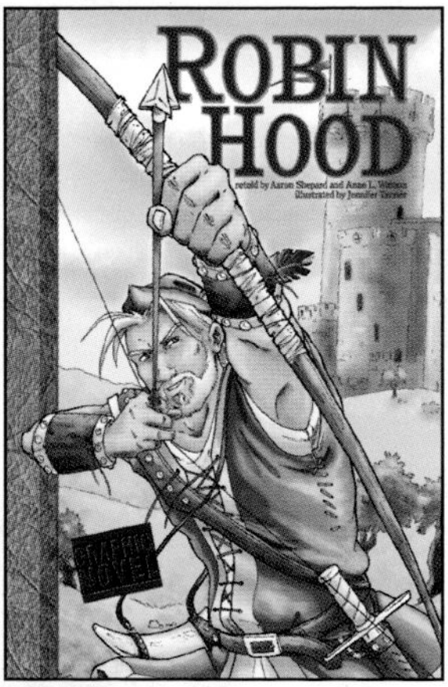
ROBIN HOOD

Robin Hood

Robin Hood and his Merrie Men are the heroes of Sherwood Forest. Taking from the rich and giving to the poor, Robin Hood and his loyal followers fight for the downtrodden and oppressed. As they outwit the cruel Sheriff of Nottingham, Robin Hood and his Merrie Men are led on a series of exciting adventures.

GRAPHIC REVOLVE

If you have enjoyed this story, there are many more exciting tales for you to discover in the Graphic Revolve collection...

20,000 Leagues Under the Sea
Black Beauty
Dracula
Frankenstein
Gulliver's Travels
The Hound of the Baskervilles
The Hunchback of Notre Dame
King Arthur and the Knights of the Round Table
Robin Hood
The Strange Case of Dr Jekyll and Mr Hyde
Treasure Island
The War of the Worlds